Understanding Excel Spreadsheets For Everyone

Jim Gatenby

BERNARD BABANI (publishing) LTD
The Grampians
Shepherds Bush Road
London W6 7NF
England

www.babanibooks.com

D1633844

Please Note

Although every care has been taken with the production of this book to ensure that any projects, designs, modifications and/or programs, etc., contained herewith, operate in a correct and safe manner and also that any components specified are normally available in Great Britain, the Publishers and Author do not accept responsibility in any way for the failure (including fault in design) of any project, design, modification or program to work correctly or to cause damage to any equipment that it may be connected to or used in conjunction with, or in respect of any other damage or injury that may be so caused, nor do the Publishers accept responsibility in any way for the failure to obtain specified components.

Notice is also given that if equipment that is still under warranty is modified in any way or used or connected with home-built equipment then that warranty may be void.

First Published – October 2016

British Library Cataloguing in Publication Data:

A catalogue record for this book is available from the British Library

ISBN 978-0-85934-765-5

Printed and bound in Great Britain for Bernard Babani (publishing) Ltd

About this Book

Microsoft Excel is the leading software for working with tables of data and producing graphs and charts. New versions of Excel have been developed for the latest smartphones and tablets, as well as the more traditional desktop and laptop computers. Together with "cloud" storage systems such as OneDrive, you can now access spreadsheets on any computer, including smartphones and tablets, in any location where there is Internet access.

This book is intended to help newcomers to spreadsheets to learn the basic skills, using simple, clear, everyday examples. A step-by-step approach is used, developed over the author's many years of teaching students of all ages.

Early chapters in the book show what you can do with Excel and introduce the latest versions, including Excel 2016 and the mobile versions. Also the Office 365 software suite including Excel and OneDrive cloud storage.

The book then covers the basic tasks of entering data, and performing calculations. The easy editing of Excel spreadsheets by amending data and inserting and deleting rows and columns is discussed, together with formatting in different styles and colours. Also the effortless creation of meaningful graphs and charts to display information clearly. The saving of files in OneDrive in the clouds and locally on your device are covered, plus printing from all types of computer including smartphones and tablets.

Important management tasks, such as deleting, renaming, moving and restoring files are discussed in detail.

Text-based worksheets such as to-do lists, which can be sorted and filtered, are discussed. Also the use of Excel as a data source for printing standard letters and address labels.

About the Author

Jim Gatenby trained as a Chartered Mechanical Engineer and initially worked at Rolls-Royce Ltd using computers in the analysis of jet engine performance. He obtained a Master of Philosophy degree in Mathematical Education by research at Loughborough University of Technology and taught mathematics and computing in school for many years before becoming a full-time author. His most recent teaching posts included Head of Computer Studies and Information Technology Coordinator. The author has written many books in the fields of educational computing and Microsoft Windows, including many of the titles in the highly successful Older Generation series from Bernard Babani (publishing) Ltd.

The author has considerable experience of teaching students of all ages and abilities, in school and in adult education. For several years he successfully taught the well-established CLAIT course and also GCSE Computing and Information Technology.

Trademarks

Microsoft Windows, Office 365, OneDrive, Word and Excel are either trademarks or registered trademarks of Microsoft Corporation. All other brand and product names used in this book are recognized as trademarks or registered trademarks, of their respective companies.

Acknowledgements

I would like to thank my wife Jill for her help and support during the writing of this book.

Contents

A Brief Introduction

Anyone Can Use a Spreadsheet

This chapter gives a general overview of spreadsheets. Later chapters give step-by-step instructions, in plain English, for the creation of various types of spreadsheet.

Many people are put off using computers because they think you have to be particularly good at maths or electronics — something of a "geek" or a "nerd", to use the modern terminology. Understanding computers is not helped by the need to grapple with strange new jargon such as *Uniform Resource Locator* (*URL*). This simply means the address of some pages of information on the worldwide network of computers known as the Internet.

As a former Maths teacher I have lost count of the number of times I've heard the expressions "I can't do Maths". However, the basic maths skills needed to manage your personal finances effectively or to estimate the cost of new business ventures are vital to survive and prosper in the modern world. As someone once said "I hate Maths… but I love counting money." The computer spreadsheet is the perfect tool for managing lists and tables of figures with ease — the computer does everything for you, as discussed throughout this book.

The spreadsheet is not just a tool for specialists such as accountants, statisticians and scientists, etc. It can be used by anyone to manage their affairs easily.

What is a Spreadsheet?

The spreadsheet is usually a table of numbers with row and column headings, as shown below. A single page is known as a *worksheet*, while several related pages are known as a *workbook*. The *software* or set of instructions needed to create and manage a spreadsheet is known as a *spreadsheet app* (application) or *spreadsheet program*. Microsoft Excel is the world's leading spreadsheet program. As shown below, you can type numbers and letters into a box or *cell*. A spreadsheet can also consist entirely of a *list* of text such as names and addresses.

◢	A	B	C	D
1		Jan	Feb	Mar
2		£	£	£
3	Shopping	480	560	550
4	Petrol	170	165	180
5	Heating	120	125	110
6	Total	770	850	840

Just Tap or Click an Icon

After entering the data you might, for example, simply tap or click the **AutoSum** icon, shown on the right. This appears on a *ribbon* or menu bar across the top of the screen, as shown below.

The column or row is totalled for you in an instant. Similar operations such as subtraction, multiplication, division and averages, etc., can also be carried out easily.

The History of Spreadsheets

Spreadsheets evolved from hand written ledgers such as accounts and balance sheets, etc. As discussed shortly, spreadsheets are now used for many different purposes such as monitoring personal health and fitness and also sporting records. The first computerised spreadsheet program, VisiCalc, was developed at Harvard University in 1978. VisiCalc was a huge success with the business world and was followed in 1983 by Lotus 1-2-3. This was also extremely popular for many years but was eventually overtaken by Microsoft Excel, on which this book is based.

Spreadsheets were first used on Apple and IBM-PC desktop computers from the late 1970's onwards. More recently Microsoft introduced mobile versions of *Excel*. So the software can now be used on tablets and smartphones, *on the move* in different locations, as well as in the home or office on laptop and desktop computers.

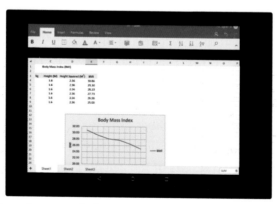

An Excel spreadsheet on a tablet computer

As discussed later, Excel makes it easy to create graphs and charts such as the line graph shown on the tablet above.

The Overall Process

The following steps are involved in obtaining and using a spreadsheet program.

Installing the Software

The *software* or *program*, also known as an *app*, is the set of instructions that control the process of creating and using a spreadsheet. The software may be bought on a CD, or downloaded from the Internet, perhaps from your computer's own *App Store*. Follow the manufacturer's instructions to permanently install the software. An *icon* or a listing in a *menu* will be placed on your screen to allow you to quickly launch the program at any time in the future.

Using the Spreadsheet Program

- Launch or run the program. You can start with a screen consisting of empty cells or boxes. Or you can use a *template* as discussed on the next page.

- *Enter* your rows and columns of data. *Format* the numbers with different letter styles, colours, etc.

- *Edit* the data to correct any mistakes.

- Carry out any *calculations*.

- *Save* the spreadsheet table as a *file* on the Internal Storage of your computer or in the Internet "clouds".

- Study the *results* of the calculations on the screen.

- *Print* all or part of the spreadsheet table on paper.

- *Insert* the spreadsheet into a report or presentation.

- *Share* a copy of the spreadsheet with someone else by sending it via the "clouds", i.e. the Internet.

Excel Templates

When you launch Excel, you can start with a blank *worksheet*. Then enter your row and column headings and the numbers and text for the data itself. The worksheet can be formatted by changing the *font*, i.e. style of lettering, and the layout and by adding various borders, lines and colours.

Alternatively Excel provides a variety of *templates* or ready-made spreadsheets, as shown below. These provide the headings, layout and design features for sheets on various subjects. You then simply enter your own text and numbers.

Ready-made spreadsheet templates

Security: The Clouds

The "clouds" are actually powerful computers connected to the Internet. If you save important spreadsheet files in *cloud storage systems* such as Microsoft OneDrive, Google Drive and Dropbox, the files will be securely managed and backed up by computer professionals, as discussed in detail later.

You can access your spreadsheets in the clouds from different computers, e.g. at work, at home or when travelling. Also send a copy of a spreadsheet to someone else via the clouds and the Internet, as discussed later.

Spreadsheet Tasks

Some typical spreadsheet tasks are as follows:

- Monitoring your weekly or monthly expenses.
- Checking your savings or shares, etc.
- Keeping track of sales in a small business.
- Recording and monitoring your health such as weight, blood pressure, BMI (Body Mass Index).
- Monitoring your fitness and performance in exercises such as running and cycling—times, heart rate, etc.
- Analysing the results of surveys, questionnaires.
- Evaluating average scores in various sports.
- Comparing students' marks in different subjects.
- Create a text-only list such as names and addresses. This can be sorted into order and used to print address labels, for example.
- Making a to-do list and labelling completed tasks.
- Modelling or "What if?" speculation. E.g. "What if inflation were to reach 10%?" or "What if the standard rate of VAT were changed to 25%?"

Recalculation — What if?

As mentioned above, you might have a list of prices with VAT calculated at 20%. To calculate the VAT at 25%, say, you simply enter the new rate and the entire spreadsheet is automatically recalculated instantly, even if there are hundreds or thousands of numbers to be amended.

Replication

This is one of the reasons why the spreadsheet is so powerful. You would click or tap the **AutoSum** button to total column **B** and produce the total **770** in cell **B6** shown below.

	A	B	C	D
1		Jan	Feb	Mar
2		£	£	£
3	Shopping	480	560	550
4	Petrol	170	165	180
5	Heating	120	125	110
6	Total	770		
7				

The totalling operation can be repeated in columns **C** and **D** by dragging along row **6** using a mouse, as shown above. The method of replication is similar but slightly different for touchscreen operation and this is discussed in detail later. A big spreadsheet can have hundreds or even thousands of rows and columns. So replication can be used to save hours of tedious manual calculation.

Graphs and Charts

Setting up the scales for graphs with pencil and paper can be difficult and time-consuming. Excel does these tasks automatically to display graphs and charts as shown below.

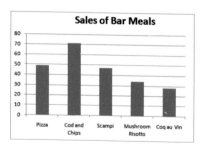

Summary

- You don't need to be a technical wizard to use a spreadsheet. The computer does the work for you at the tap or click of a button.

- Spreadsheets can save hours of work. Enter a calculation once then *replicate* it by dragging along rows or down columns.

- A spreadsheet can be edited easily, updated with the latest data and *recalculated* automatically. This allows "What if?" prediction of future outcomes.

- A spreadsheet can be instantly *sorted* into alphabetical or numerical order.

- Ready-made *templates* allow professional-looking spreadsheets to be created and printed or shared.

- Tables of figures can be converted to attractive *graphs and charts* very quickly and easily.

- An Excel spreadsheet can be easily imported into a *report* or a *presentation* for a meeting.

- An Excel spreadsheet can be used to store a text-only list, such as names and addresses. This can then act as the *data source* to print standard letters and address labels in a word processor.

- Mobile versions of Excel enable spreadsheets to be accessed *on the move* on tablets and smartphones.

- Internet *cloud storage* allows spreadsheets to be accessed from anywhere, on any type of computer.

2
Versions of Excel

Introduction

The last chapter was intended to show that a spreadsheet is simply a table of text and numbers. Unlike traditional tables of figures created using pen/pencil and paper, spreadsheet software such as Microsoft Excel does all the arduous mathematical work for you, at the touch of a button. Excel also helps you to interpret sets of figures by easily producing clear and attractive graphs and charts.

Microsoft Excel was first introduced in 1985 on the Apple Macintosh, followed by the Windows version in 1987. Numerous new versions of Excel were produced over the intervening years until the latest edition, Excel 2016.

Microsoft Office

As discussed shortly, the latest version of the Excel spreadsheet program, Excel 2016, can be purchased separately or as part of an Office 2016 suite of software. The suite may also include other leading business programs such as Microsoft Word and Microsoft Access.

In addition, you can buy Excel as part of a cloud-based suite known as Office 365. This is paid for by subscription and can be installed on several machines — PC or Mac, tablet or phone. Office 365 provides *1 TB* (see page 14) of storage space using the ***OneDrive cloud storage*** system.

Excel on Different Platforms

Initially Excel was used on PC and Mac desktop and laptop computers. Recent years have seen the development of powerful new handheld tablet computers and smartphones. As a result *mobile* versions of Excel have been developed for these handheld devices. The versions of Excel designed for the mobile tablets and smartphones, although somewhat simplified, have all the main core features of Excel 2016.

Horses for Courses

Many of us now use all of the main computer platforms at various times — desktop and laptop computers, tablets and smartphones. For example, if you were setting up a computer to do serious amounts of number crunching in an office you would be better off with a desktop machine with it's large screen and keyboard and ergonomic layout.

However, the smaller tablets and smartphones are essential for computing on the move. It's quite feasible to read spreadsheets and charts on hand-held devices and also carry out small amounts of data entry and editing. You might create spreadsheets on PCs or Macs at home or work, then view or discuss the same spreadsheets and charts on tablets or smartphones while on the move, away from your base.

OneDrive

Excel and Office 365 are closely associated with OneDrive. OneDrive, discussed in detail later, is a cloud storage system using professionally managed Internet server computers. These make it possible to access your Excel and other files on any computer in any location where there is an Internet connection.

Excel Everywhere

If you use several types of computer, as shown below, a spreadsheet can be created and saved on any one of them. It can then be exported to any of your other computers, where it can be viewed, edited and saved, if necessary.

Desktop or laptop PC or Mac

Tablet
(Android, iPad, Windows)

Smartphone
(Android, iPhone, Windows)

Minimum Requirements for Excel Versions

Version of Excel	Operating System
Excel 2016	
Windows PC or laptop	Windows 7 or higher
Windows tablet	Windows 8 or higher
Mac	Mac OS X 10.10
Excel Mobile	
Windows tablet and phone	Windows 10
Excel for Android	
Android tablet and phone	KitKat 4.4 or later ARM-based processor or Intel x86 processor 1GB RAM or above
Excel for iPad, etc.	
iPad/iPhone	iOS 8.0 or higher
iPad Pro	iOS 9.0 or higher

Jargon

- The *operating system (OS)* is the *program* i.e. *set of instructions*, controlling the running of a computer.

- The *processor* is a chip known as the "brains" of a computer, carrying out instructions and calculations.

- The *RAM* is the temporary *memory* inside of a computer used to store *programs* and *data*.

- 1 *GB* or *Gigabyte* is the memory needed to store roughly *1,000,000,000* letters, characters, or digits 0-9.

Finding the Specification of a Computer

Details such as the operating system (OS), RAM, processor, etc., may be given on the packaging and documentation supplied with your device(s) or in advertisements.

For a Windows machine, right-click or hold the Windows key shown on the right. Then select **Control Panel**, **System and Security** then **System**. Then select **View amount of RAM and processor speed**. This will also show the version of Windows installed.

A *Google search* with your device name and model number should also produce the required information, as shown on page 12. In the example below, **Nexus 7 Spec** was entered into Google. The Web site **GSMARENA.com** provided the full specification, shown in part below.

PLATFORM	OS	Android OS, v4.1.2 (Jelly Bean)
	Chipset	Nvidia Tegra 3
	CPU	Quad-core 1.2 GHz Cortex-A9
	GPU	ULP GeForce
MEMORY	Card slot	No
	Internal	8/16/32 GB, 1 GB RAM

Although this particular machine had enough **RAM** to meet the required Android specification shown on page 12, the **Jelly Bean** operating system (OS) needs upgrading to KitKat 4.4 or later. Swipe down from the top of the screen and tap the **Settings** icon shown on the right. Then select **About tablet** and **System updates**. In this example **Jelly Bean (version 4.1.2)** can be upgraded to **Lollipop (version 5.1.1)**.

iPads and iPhones use the **Settings** app and then **General** and **Software Update** to view the current operating system and install a later version.

Excel 2016 as Part of Office 365

You can buy Excel 2016 as part of the *Office 365* suite, from the Microsoft Store, as shown below.

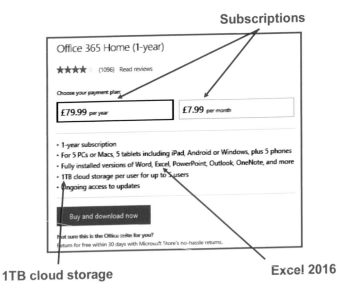

Subscriptions

1TB cloud storage   **Excel 2016**

Office 365 Home edition allows Excel 2016 and the other Office applications to be installed on up to 5 PCs or Macs, 5 tablets and 5 phones. This includes *1TB* of storage in OneDrive in the clouds. With a valid subscription you receive regular updates to the Excel 2016 software.

There are several editions of Office 365 such as *Home*, *Personal*, *Business* and *University*. These include different programs in addition to Word 2016 and Excel 2016, etc. Full details are given at **www.microsoftstore.com**.

1 *TB (Terabyte)* is the storage space needed for roughly 1,000,000,000,000 letters, characters, or digits 0-9.

Getting Office 365 on a Windows 10 PC

Click or tap the Windows button, shown on the right, at the bottom left-hand corner of the screen.

Then select the **Get Office** tile on the Start Menu, as shown on the right. The **Get more out of Office** screen opens as shown below. This includes training videos and notes to familiarise you with Office and its various apps, such as Word and Excel and OneDrive cloud storage.

You are also informed that while the free apps, such as Excel for mobile devices, allow you to do basic tasks, subscribing to Office 365 gives extra features on all types of computer.

Follow the instructions on the screen to complete your installation of the latest version of Office 365, including Excel 2016. Launching or opening Excel 2016 to start creating or editing a spreadsheet is discussed on page 26.

Advantages of Office 365

Office 365 gives you the following facilities:

- On-going *upgrades* to the latest Excel software.
- Access to Excel on all your PCs, tablets and phones.
- 1 TB of storage in the clouds.

Getting Excel 2016 Standalone for PC and Mac

The Excel 2016 program can also be bought separately online, as shown below, and downloaded from the Microsoft Store and other sources. Desktop and laptop computers need Windows 7 or later while tablets need Windows 8 or 10.

Excel 2016 for the Mac is obtained in a similar way to the PC example shown above. Mac OS X 10.10 is required. The standalone version of Excel 2016 does not have the advantages of Office 365 listed above.

Getting Office 2016 for PC and Mac

You can download a copy of Office 2016, which includes Excel 2016, from the Microsoft Store at :

www.microsoftstore.com/UK/Office-2016

Office 2016 is also available from other suppliers such as Amazon and PC World. You will normally buy a package including a ***product key*** (rather than a DVD), allowing you to download and install the software.

Office 2016 differs from Office 365, discussed on the previous pages, as follows:

- Office 2016 is bought with a single, one-off payment.
- A product key only allows Office 2016 to be installed on a *single PC* or *Mac*, not several devices.
- Office 2016 has only *15GB* of free OneDrive cloud storage, not the *1TB* available to users of Office 365.
- Office 2016 does not get regular updates to software such as Excel.

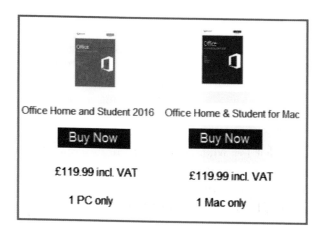

Launching Excel 2016

An icon for Excel 2016 is placed on the **All apps** menu, as shown on the left below.

To launch, i.e. open, Excel 2016, click or tap the **Windows** icon shown on the right. Then select the **All apps** icon on the **Start Menu**, as shown on the right above. Then select **Excel 2016** shown on the left above. The start-up screen shown below opens, allowing you to:

- Create a spreadsheet from a blank page.
- Create a spreadsheet using a ready-made template.
- Open an existing saved spreadsheet.

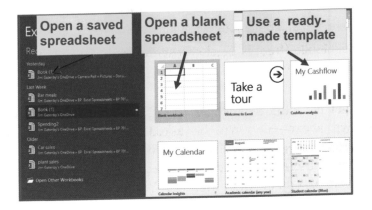

Excel Mobile

This is designed for creating, editing and viewing spreadsheets on Windows phones and tablets with a diagonal screen size of 10.1inches or smaller. This has all the core features of Excel 2016, enabling you to access spreadsheets on the move on various types of device.

Open the Windows Store from its tile on the Start Menu, shown on the right. Then enter **Excel** in the Search bar at the top of the Windows Store and tap the search icon to display **Excel Mobile** as shown below.

Tap the **Excel Mobile** icon shown above, then tap **INSTALL**.

Excel Mobile (free) is quickly installed and you can then tap **OPEN** to view a choice of opening screens, very similar to those listed on page 18.

To get the extra advantages of Office 365, tap **Get Office** shown above. You will be asked to sign in with your Microsoft account name and password and if necessary start a new subscription, as discussed earlier. A **Get Office** tile also appears on the Start Menu of Windows 10.

Excel for Android

You can use Excel on an Android tablet, smartphone or *hybrid* (a tablet with a separate keyboard, also known as a *2-in-1* computer). A *free* copy of Microsoft Excel can be downloaded and installed from the Play Store, opened after tapping the icon shown on the right.

Enter **Excel** in the Play Store search bar to display the icon shown below. Then tap **READ MORE** for more information or tap **INSTALL** to copy Excel to your device.

Microsoft Excel ⋮
Microsoft Corporation

4.4 ★

The installation process, as shown below, only takes a minute or two and you can then tap **OPEN** to start using Excel on your Android device.

Microsoft Excel
Microsoft Corporation ✧
▣ PEGI 3

21.21 MB/55.42MB   **38%** ✕

In-app purchases

Microsoft Excel for Android devices is free, but **In-app purchases** shown at the bottom right of the previous page indicates that there are extra features which may require a payment.

The installation process places an icon for **Excel** on the Apps Screen of your Android device, as shown below. Tap the icon whenever you want to start using Excel.

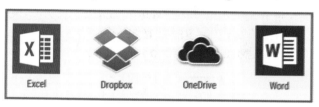

OneDrive, shown above, is a *cloud storage* system and very relevant to Excel. OneDrive, discussed in detail in Chapter 10, allows you to access all your Excel spreadsheets on *different types of computer* from *different locations*, via the Internet.

Launching Excel for Android

Tap the **Excel** icon shown above. If you have a subscription to Office 365, as discussed earlier, sign in to your Microsoft account to access all the features of Excel and Office, as discussed earlier.

Next the start-up screen opens, very similar to that shown at the bottom of page 18, with the same start-up options, as shown below.

- Create a spreadsheet from a blank page.
- Create a spreadsheet using a ready-made template.
- Open an existing saved spreadsheet.

Excel for iOS (iPad and iPhone)

Tap the App Store icon shown on the right and enter **Excel** in the Search bar. Then tap **Search** on the keyboard to display the **Microsoft Excel** listing in the App Store, as shown below.

App Store

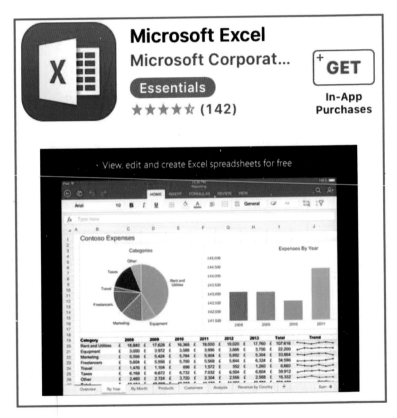

Tap **Details** and **Reviews** for more information. Or tap **GET** then **INSTALL** to begin downloading and installing Excel.

The installation is complete when the circle shown on the near right has completely changed to a thick blue line, as shown on the far right. Now tap **OPEN**. A number of screens giving information about Excel are given. E.g. changes to spreadsheets are *saved automatically* if you have *AutoSave* switched on in Excel, as discussed later.

There is also an option to sign in to an existing Microsoft account, on your iPad or IPhone, as shown below.

If the Microsoft account has a valid subscription to Office 365, you will be able to *create* and *edit* spreadsheets and use the additional features of Office 365, as listed on page 14. If you choose the **Sign In Later** option shown above, you may only be able to *view* spreadsheets on your iPad or iPhone. You can buy Office 365 from the Microsoft Store, as discussed on page 14.

Launching Excel for iPad and iPhone

Tap the new **Excel** icon on your Apps screen, as shown on the right. The start-up options are broadly the same as those shown on page 18.

Summary: Versions of Excel

- Microsoft Excel is the world's leading software for creating and editing spreadsheets and charts.

- *Excel 2016* is the latest version for PCs and Macs. This can be bought separately or as component part of the *Office 365* software suite.

- There are several versions of Office 365, e.g. for *home*, *business* and *student users*.

- Office 365 can be bought by monthly or yearly *subscription* and gives benefits such as *1TB* of cloud storage and *automatic updates* to Excel.

- Depending on the subscription plan chosen, you can install Office 365 on *multiple devices* such as Desktop PCs and Macs. Also tablets and phones such as Androids and iOS (iPads and iPhones).

- Free Excel apps are available in the appropriate app store for mobile devices with screen sizes less than 10.1 inches. These give the essential features for creating, viewing and editing spreadsheets.

- *OneDrive cloud computing* enables spreadsheets to be viewed anywhere, at home, at the office or on the move, on any type of computer.

- The mobile versions of Excel are more limited than Excel 2016, yet capable of the essential functions. Excel 2016 spreadsheet files can be imported into the mobile versions of Excel but without some of the advanced formatting features.

Finding Your Way Around Excel

Introduction

The previous chapter discussed obtaining and installing the various versions of Excel, from *Excel 2016* for PCs and Macs to the *mobile* versions for tablets and smartphones. All of these versions operate in a broadly similar way and so in the remainder of this book the term Excel on its own will refer to all the versions. Where there are differences, such as the contents of the *ribbon* across the top of the screen, these will be discussed in the text.

This chapter introduces the main tools in Excel for creating spreadsheets, such as the ribbon and the *formula bar.*

Later chapters give more detailed, step-by-step instructions for creating, formatting, saving, editing and printing spreadsheets and also graphs and charts.

Terms Used in this Book

Throughout this book, the terms *spreadsheet* and *worksheet* are both used to mean a table of *cells* in labelled rows and columns, which may contain numbers, words and formulas.

A *workbook* has several spreadsheets or worksheets in layers and saved as a single *file.* Sheets are accessed via tabs at the bottom left of the screen as **Sheet1, Sheet2**, etc.

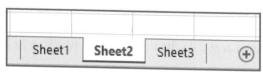

Launching Excel

On a tablet or phone tap the icon for Excel on your Apps screen, as shown on the right.

On Windows machines tap or click the Windows button and select **All apps** as discussed on page 18. Then select **Excel 2016** or **Excel Mobile** as shown below.

(My Windows 10 PC and Windows 10 tablet run both Excel Mobile and Excel 2016).

Excel Mobile was primarily designed for machines with a screen size of less than 10.1 inches, but it can also be run on larger PCs and laptops.

Excel opens with options to start a new, blank workbook, or take a tour of Excel, or use a ready-made template — a worksheet design into which you can add your own data.

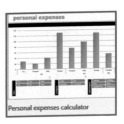

The Worksheet

Shown below is an almost blank *worksheet*. A *workbook* may contain several worksheets or spreadsheets, known as *Sheet1*, *Sheet2*, etc., as shown on page 25.

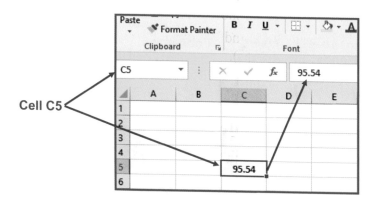

The worksheet is actually a grid of boxes, known as *cells*. Each cell has a unique *cell reference*, such as **C5** shown above, defined by its *column* and *row headers* in this case **C** and **5**, built into Excel. A worksheet can extend to thousands of rows and thousands of columns, far more than most people would ever need.

Tap or click to select a cell. Then you can enter:

- *Labels*, e.g. **Name**, **Wage**, **Price**, etc.
- *Numbers*, e.g. **95.54** shown above.
- *Formulas*, e.g. **=SUM(C5:C8)**.

A cell can be formatted with different *fonts* (or styles of lettering) and also *cell borders* and *fill colours*.

The Excel 2016 Ribbon

Excel 2016, like Word 2016, is operated by a *ribbon* as shown in part below. The ribbon has a number of *tabs*, such as **File**, **Home**, and **Insert** shown below. Each tab displays groups of icons for various tasks.

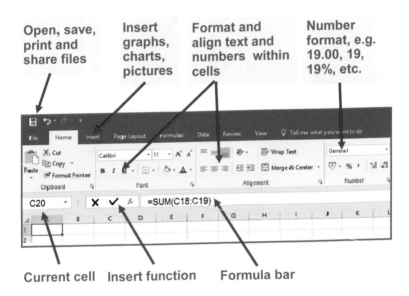

The above screenshot shows some of the essential tools for creating and editing a spreadsheet and these are discussed in more detail shortly when we start creating a worksheet.

The centre of the Excel 2016 ribbon is occupied by some very sophisticated cell formatting colours and styles, not shown here. These features are discussed later in this book.

Shown on the next page is the right-hand side of the Excel 2016 ribbon with some of the most commonly used tools labelled.

Insert cells, rows, columns

Delete cells, rows, columns

Sort into order or filter out some numbers

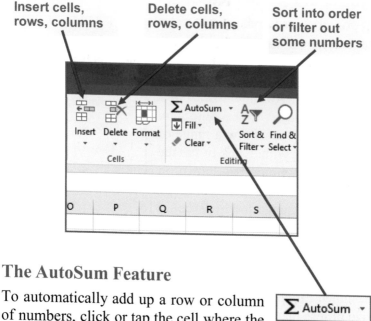

The AutoSum Feature

To automatically add up a row or column of numbers, click or tap the cell where the Σ AutoSum total is to appear. Then click or tap the Σ icon. In the example below, Excel assumes you want to add cells **B3** to **B6**, enclosed by dotted lines, and automatically inserts the *formula* **=SUM(B3:B6)**. (In Excel the **=** sign denotes a formula). The **AutoSum** feature is discussed in more detail shortly.

	A	B
1		
2		
3		19
4		35
5		52
6		65
7		=SUM(B3:B6)

The Average Function

If you click or tap the small arrow to the right of **AutoSum** shown on the right, Excel 2016 displays a menu, including **Average** shown on the right. **Average** works in a similar way to **AutoSum**, automatically assuming a range of cells to work with. Click or tap the tick on the formula bar shown on page 31 to accept the cell range and formula suggested by Excel 2016.

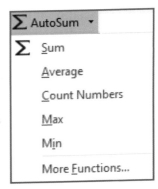

The Ribbon on Mobile Versions of Excel

As discussed in Chapter 2, versions of Excel have been designed for tablets and smartphones with a diagonal screen size of less than 10.1 ins. These have a much simpler ribbon than Excel 2016, while still having the essential spreadsheet features. One difference is that the mobile versions have fewer choices for formatting cells and text.

Excel for Android Ribbon

The ribbons for all of the mobile versions of Excel are essentially the same as the Android ribbon shown above.

Formula Bars

The formula bars for Excel 2016 and the mobile versions of Excel are shown below. Although different in appearance their features are basically the same.

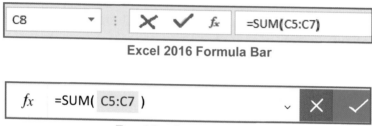

Excel 2016 Formula Bar

Excel for Android Formula Bar

The iPad and iPhone formula bars are very similar to the Android bar shown above.

Operations such as **Sum** and **Average** can be accessed from the **AutoSum** icon on the ribbon, as discussed on pages 29 and 30. For example, if you select **AutoSum** and **Sum** shown on page 30, a formula such as **=SUM(C5:C7)** would appear in the formula bar, as shown above.

The above formula means "add up all the numbers in the range of cells from **C5** to **C7** inclusive".

If you're happy with the formula click or tap the tick, as shown in the two formula bars above. Otherwise select the cross and edit the formula by typing in the formula bar.

When you select the tick, the answer, not the formula appears in the currently selected cell on the worksheet.

Although very simple examples are given here, in practise a spreadsheet can easily be used to do calculations on hundreds of rows or columns.

Entering Your Own Formulas

As well as the functions such as **SUM** and **AVERAGE** built into Excel, you can also type a formula of your own into the formula bar.

First select the cell on the worksheet where you want the answer to appear. Then type = and start entering the formula.

These use the following signs as mathematical operators:

+ addition

- subtraction

* multiplication

/ division

These might be used as follows, by typing into the formula bar. The answer appears in the cell where the formula is entered, after you've selected the tick on the formula bar, as shown on page 31.

=D6+D7+D8	Add the contents of cells **D6** to **D8**
=F9-F8	Subtract cell **F8** from cell **F9**
=C6*D6	Multiply cell **C6** by cell **D6**
=E10/D10	Divide cell **E10** by cell **D10**
=G10*1.20	Multiply cell **G10** by **1.20**, e.g. to increase the contents of **G10** by **20%**
=M39*0.20	Multiply cell **M39** by **0.20**, e.g. to calculate the VAT at **20%** on the price of an article).

Further Functions

Many users of Excel may find the basic built-in functions such as **AutoSum, Sum** and **Average** will cover many of their requirements. These can also be supplemented by typing your own formulas into the formula bar as shown on the previous page. Also, as mentioned previously, a spreadsheet can simply be used for creating text-only sheets, such as *to-do lists* or *address lists*.

However, Excel is also extremely useful for more advanced scientific and professional work and provides a range of built-in functions, shown in the small sample below. These can be accessed after tapping the **Insert Function** button on the formula bar, as shown on the right and on page 31.

Insert function

Once you've entered a formula into a cell, you can easily *replicate* the same formula across many columns or down many rows. Excel automatically adjusts the cell references in each *calculated cell*. This can save an enormous amount of time compared with traditional methods of calculation with pencil and paper, etc..

Mouse Versus Touchscreen

Excel 2016

This is currently the most powerful version of Excel and is mainly intended for use on desktop machines with a mouse and laptop machines with a *touchpad.* The touchpad, not to be confused with the touchscreen, is operated in a very similar way to a mouse. However, some desktop and laptop machines are supplied with a *touchscreen monitor.* Also some powerful tablets can run Excel 2016.

So Excel 2016 can be used with both mouse and touchscreen operation on suitable devices.

Mobile Versions of Excel

These versions include *Excel Mobile* for Windows tablets and smartphones. Mobile versions for Android, iPad and iPhone are known in their respective app stores simply as *Microsoft Excel.* These mobile versions of Excel are designed mainly for use with touchscreen tablets and phones with a screen size of less than 10.1inches.

However, *Bluetooth* wireless mice and separate keyboards are available for Android and Windows tablets and phones. Mice and keyboards are also available for iPads and iPhones. So the mobile versions of Excel can be operated either with the usual touchscreen or with a mouse on a tablet, smartphone or *hybrid* computer. The hybrid ("a tablet that thinks it's a laptop"), has a touchscreen and also an attachable/detachable keyboard which includes a built-in touchpad.

Therefore all versions of Excel can be operated with both mouse and touchscreen, as discussed in the next few pages.

Excel Mouse Operations

Click

(A single press of the left button).

- Selects a single cell.
- Selects a tool icon from the ribbon, e.g. to switch on a formatting feature.
- Opens a menu, e.g. the **File** menu on the ribbon, with options such as **Save** or **Print** a worksheet.
- Selects an option from a menu.
- Click in a row or column *header* to select, i.e. highlight, the entire row or column.

Double-click

(Two clicks in quick succession)

Selects a cell and displays a flashing cursor, ready for the entry of data (numbers or labels) or a formula.

Right-click

(A single press of the right-hand mouse button)

Right-click in a cell or a group of selected cells to open a menu with options such as to **Cut**, **Copy** and **Format** cells. Right-click in a row or column *header* to apply menu options to all of the cells in a row or column.

As shown on the next page, the Excel 2016 menu has an extensive list of options and a pop-up formatting bar at the top. This allows you to format text, numbers and cell borders. Mobile versions of Excel have much slimmer menus, as shown on page 38.

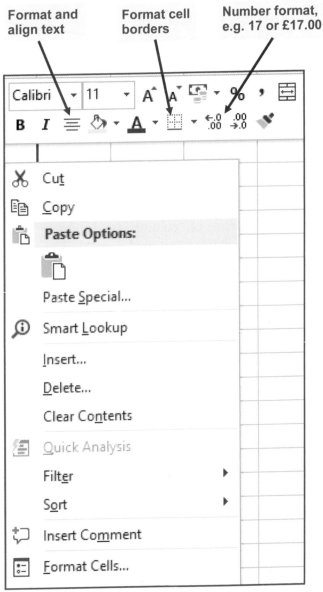

Format and align text

Format cell borders

Number format, e.g. 17 or £17.00

Excel 2016

Drag and Drop with a Mouse

Click and hold the left button then drag across the screen and finally release the button. On a touchpad, hold down the left button and slide a finger across the pad surface.

Selecting a Group of Cells Using Drag and Drop

The selected cells are highlighted as shown below.

	Jan	Feb	Mar
	£	£	£
Shopping	480	560	550
Petrol	170	165	180
Heating	120	125	110

The selected cells can then be edited or formatted using the menu shown on the previous page, after right-clicking in the selected area.

Replication

Drag and drop can also be used in *replication* in which a formula in a *calculated cell* is applied to all the other cells in a row or column. This is discussed in detail in Chapter 4.

Scrolling

Use the *scroll wheel* on the mouse, or drag the horizontal *scroll bars* at the edges of the screen, to display different areas of a large worksheet on the screen.

Zoom In and Zoom Out

Keeping the **Control** key held down, turn the scroll wheel on the mouse, to zoom in or out of the worksheet.

Excel Touchscreen Gestures

Tap

(A quick press with the finger or a stylus).

- Has the same uses as a single click with a mouse, as listed at the top of page 35.

- In addition, tapping in a row or column header displays a menu, as shown below. These options apply to a *whole row or column*.

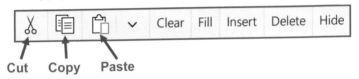

Cut   Copy   Paste

Double-tap

(Two taps in quick succession)

Displays a cursor for entering and editing data in cell. Also displays the on-screen keyboard.

Hold and release

Similar to the menu shown above, this action displays a menu, shown below, to **Cut**, **Copy**, and **Paste** and **Clear** the contents of a *single cell*. **Fill** allows you to copy the contents of a cell into multiple cells in a selected area.

Android

iPad and iPhone

Drag and Drop with a Touchscreen

When you tap to select a cell, two circles appear, as shown on the right.

Selecting Cells

Touch and hold then *slide* one of the circles shown above to select or highlight a group of cells, as shown on page 37. The selected cells can then be edited and formatted, etc. The lower menus shown on page 38 appears with options including **Cut**, **Copy** and **Paste** the selected group of cells.

Replication

The **Fill** command shown on the previous page can be used can be used for *replication*. This takes a formula in a *calculated cell* and applies it to all the other cells in a row or column, allowing for changes in the cell references. So, for example, **=SUM(B3:B9)** would be replicated as **=SUM (C3:C9)**, **=SUM(D3:D9)**, **=SUM(E3:E9)**, etc. This is discussed in detail on page 45.

Scrolling

Touch and hold a cell then *slide* the finger across the screen in any direction to scroll the worksheet to display different areas of a large worksheet on the screen.

Zoom in and Zoom Out

With two fingers touching the screen, *pinch* or draw them together to make all the cells smaller, i.e. zoom out. *Stretch* the fingers apart to make the cells bigger, i.e. zoom in.

Summary:
Finding Your Way Around Excel

- An Excel Workbook can include several *layered* spreadsheets or worksheets, accessed by *tabs*.

- Excel can start with a *blank worksheet*, a *guided tour* or a ready-made *template* for the entry of your data.

- The worksheet is a grid of cells, referred to by their *column* letter and *row* number, such as **C5**.

- A cell can contain *words*, *numbers* or a *formula* to insert a calculated result in the cell.

- The *ribbon* across the top of the screen contains icons and tabs for formatting, etc., and menus for major tasks such as saving and printing.

- The *formula bar* can be used to enter and edit formulas and to insert them into a *calculated cell*. All formulas start with **=**, as in **=SUM(C7:C13)**.

- The **Insert Function** key allows you to select ready-made formulas relating to many different subjects.

- The mobile versions of Excel are slimmed down versions of Excel 2016 but still have the essential features for creating and editing large spreadsheets.

- Excel 2016 and the mobile versions of Excel can all be operated by *touchscreen gestures* on suitable devices. Alternatively, if you prefer, you can use a *mouse* or a *touchpad* or *trackball*.

Creating a Spreadsheet

Introduction

The work which follows has been tested on all types of computer platform — desktop, laptop, tablet and phone. The work also covers all of the main computer *operating systems*, Windows 10, Android and iOS (iPad and iPhone).

So the text in the remainder of this book applies to all of these platforms unless stated otherwise. Where there are significant differences these are explained in the text.

This work is intended to show that Excel spreadsheet files created on one type of computer can be viewed, edited and printed using any other type of device. This *portability* requires that the user of each machine is signed into a Microsoft account which is associated with a valid subscription to Office 365, as discussed in Chapter 2.

For simplicity the sample spreadsheets in this book are very small, based on only a few rows and columns. However, the methods described can be just as easily applied to large spreadsheets containing hundreds or even thousands of rows and columns. This is possible because of the very powerful but easy-to-use *replication* features in Excel, discussed in detail in this chapter.

Getting Started

Launch Excel and open a blank worksheet, as discussed on page 26. You can start in any cell you like.

Double-click or double-tap to select a cell with a flashing cursor, ready to start entering the data, such as the small sheet shown below. On a tablet or phone the on-screen keyboard appears when you first double-tap. Enter the data in a cell then press **Return** or **Enter** to move down a column. To move across the sheet click or tap the required cell.

◢	A	B	C	D	E
1					
2					
3			Jan	Feb	Mar
4			£	£	£
5		Shopping	480	560	550
6		Petrol	170	165	180
7		Heating	120	125	110
8		Total			

Formatting the labels and numbers is discussed later.

If you make a mistake when entering or editing data, the **Undo** icon shown below allows you to recover the situation.

The Undo Icon

To cancel the last action(s), click or tap the **Undo** icon on the ribbon, as shown on the right.

The Redo Icon

To reverse the undo operation, click or tap the **Redo** icon on the ribbon, as shown on the right.

Totalling the Columns

Select cell **C8** shown on page 42. Then select the **AutoSum** icon, shown on the right, on the ribbon. On Androids, tap the **AutoSum** icon then select **SUM** from the menu which drops down. On iOS (iPads and iPhones) select the **Formulas** tab, then tap the **AutoSum** icon and then select **SUM** from the drop-down menu..

Excel assumes a range of cells that you wish to total, as shown outlined in blue below.

	Jan	Feb
	£	£
Shopping	480	560
Petrol	170	165
Heating	120	125
Total	=SUM(C5:C7)	

If the range of cells is correct, select the tick in the formula bar as shown below. Otherwise, you can either:

      Drag the rectangle using the handles, as shown above.

Or: Edit the range by typing in the formula bar.

Excel 2016 Formula Bar

Excel for Android Formula Bar

Alternatively, click the cross shown above to clear cell **C8** and start creating the calculated cell again.

When you tick to insert a formula, the *result*, not the formula, appears in the calculated cell, **C8** in this example.

f_x	=SUM(C5:C7)			
◢	A	B	C	D	E
1					
2					
3			Jan	Feb	Mar
4			£	£	£
5		Shopping	480	560	550
6		Petrol	170	165	180
7		Heating	120	125	110
8		Total	770		
9					

When you click or tap in a calculated cell, the formula appears in the formula bar, as shown above.

Replication Along a Row

The next task is to apply the formula **=SUM(C5:C7)** in cell **C8**, shown above, to all of the other columns, i.e. cells **D8** and **E8**, taking into account the column labels **D** and **E**.

Using a Mouse for Replication

Using a mouse, hover the cursor over the bottom right of the calculated cell until a **+** sign appears.

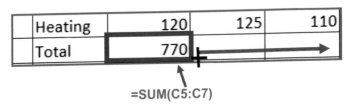

Heating	120	125	110
Total	770		

=SUM(C5:C7)

Then drag the **+** across columns **D** and **E**, as shown above, to apply the formula along the row, as shown on page 45.

Using a Touchscreen for Replication

On a touchscreen tablet or phone, etc.,

- Tap and hold in the calculated cell **C8**.
- Select **Fill** from the menu which pops up.

- *Drag* or *slide* the small square (Android) or arrow (iPads and iPhones) which appears, as shown below, across columns **D** and **E**.

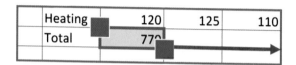

After the replication the **Totals** will appear in **D8** and **E8** as shown below.

◢	A	B	C	D	E
1					
2					
3			Jan	Feb	Mar
4			£	£	£
5		Shopping	480	560	550
6		Petrol	170	165	180
7		Heating	120	125	110
8		Total	770	850	840
9					

=SUM(D5:D7)   =SUM(E5:E7)

Cells **D8** and **E8** are *calculated cells*, displaying the *result* of the formulas **=SUM(D5:D7)** and **=SUM(E5:E7)**.

Replication Down a Column

This works in a similar way to replication along a row, just described.

- Select the cell **F5** in which the first total is to appear.
- Select **AutoSum** icon and then **Sum**, if necessary.
- Accept or adjust the range of cells assumed by Excel.
- Click or tap the tick on the formula bar to insert the formula **=SUM(C5:E5)** in cell **F5**.
- Hover or hold over the calculated cell, **F5**.
- *Replicate* the formula down column **F** by dragging or sliding as discussed on the previous two pages.
- The replicated row totals appear down column **F**, as shown below.

◢	B	C	D	E	F
1					
2					
3		Jan	Feb	Mar	Total
4		£	£	£	
5	Shopping	480	560	550	1590
6	Petrol	170	165	180	515
7	Heating	120	125	110	355
8	Total	770	850	840	2460
9					

The Power of Replication

Replication can be used to copy much more complex formulas on much larger spreadsheets, involving many more rows and columns — thus reducing many complicated calculations to a single drag with a mouse or slide with finger or stylus.

Formatting

The worksheet shown on the previous page can be improved by formatting. For example, the labels **Jan**, **Feb**, **Mar** and **Total** could be *centered*. Also the numbers could use the normal format for **£** which has 2 decimal places. The general method is to:

- Select or highlight the cells to be formatted.
- Click or tap the required formatting icon on the ribbon.

Selecting Multiple Cells

- To select all the cells along a row, click or tap in the row header such as **3** or **4** shown on the previous page.
- To select all the cells in a column, click or tap in the column header, such as **C** or **D** on the previous page.
- To select a group of cells extending over several rows and columns:

1. Using a Mouse

With a mouse, click in one of the cells of the required area, then drag the cursor to highlight the area. (Click anywhere in a cell except the bottom right -hand corner, as this will *replicate* the selected cell contents into all the other cells).

2. Using a Touchscreen

Tap a cell to display two circles, as shown on the right. Then touch and drag one of the circles to select, i.e. highlight, the required area, as shown on the next page.

◢	A	B	C	D	E	F
1						
2						
3			Jan	Feb	Mar	Total
4			£	£	£	£
5		Shopping	480.00	560.00	550.00	1,590.00
6		Petrol	170.00	165.00	180.00	515.00
7		Heating	120.00	125.00	110.00	355.00
8		Total	770.00	850.00	840.00	2,460.00
9						

In the example above, the cells shown in blue were selected by dragging from cell **C3** to **F4**. Then the icon shown on the right was selected from the ribbon, to centre the labels as shown above.

The cells highlighted in yellow were selected by dragging from cell **C5** to **F8**. Then the **Number Format** icon shown on the right was selected, followed by the icon shown on the lower right to increase the number of decimal places to 2. The **Number Format** menu is shown below.

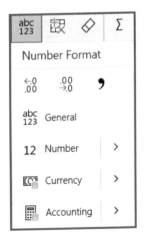

Currency on the **Number Format** on page 48 can show negative amounts in red or alternatively with a minus sign.

£1,234.10

-£1,234.10

The **Accounting** option shown on the previous menu displays the numbers with a £ sign and two decimal places, and can also be used for Euros and Dollars, as shown below.

£ 480.00

£ 170.00

£	English (United Kingdom)
€	Euro (€ 123)
$	English (United States)

Other Formatting Features

Many other formatting features are available as icons on the ribbon. These can be applied in the same way as just described, after selecting or highlighting the required cells then selecting the appropriate icon.

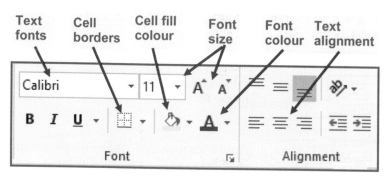

Part of the Excel 2016 Ribbon

As shown on the next page, the formatting features on mobile devices, cover all the essential features shown on the Excel 2016 ribbon above.

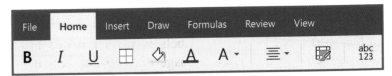

Excel for Android Ribbon

The formatting icons on iOS are very similar to the Android icons shown above. Some of the main formatting icons are discussed in detail below. (Excel 2016 formatting is discussed on pages 48 and 49). Formatting methods are basically the same on all versions of Excel.

 Display *cell borders* and select colour and line thickness for the cell borders..

 Change the *fill colour* of selected cells.

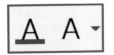 Change *font colour* and *size*.

 Change the text *alignment* — left, right justified, centered, etc.

 Apply various *cell styles*, as shown on the next page. On Excel 2016 and Excel Mobile, the **Cell Styles** appear on the right of the ribbon.

Android   **iOS**

 Select the **Number Format**, as discussed on page 48.

Cell Styles and Colours

In the worksheet below, the labels in rows 2 and 3 have been centered as discussed on page 48. The numbers have been formatted in the **Number Format** with two decimal places, also discussed on page 48.

The general method is to select or highlight the required cells or group of cells as discussed on page 47, then select the required formatting icon.

If you select one of the two **Cell Styles** icons shown on the previous page, various themes are available to apply to the selected cells. On Excel 2016 and Excel Mobile **Cell Styles** are accessed directly from the right-hand side of the ribbon. **Cell Styles** include bold text for labels and titles, etc., and either black or white text on a wide range of fill colours.

As shown below, you can change the colour and thickness of the cell borders and use different fill colours for certain cells such as row or column totals.

◢	A	B	C	D	E
1					
2		Jan	Feb	Mar	Total
3	Item	£	£	£	£
4	Shopping	480.00	560.00	550.00	1590.00
5	Petrol	170.00	165.00	180.00	515.00
6	Heating	120.00	125.00	110.00	355.00
7	Total		770.00	850.00	840.00	2460.00

Calculating Averages

The *average* of a set of numbers is a typical value, in the middle, between the extremes. The average is calculated by adding all of the numbers together and dividing by the number of numbers. With a large set of numbers this is a very tedious task to do by hand. With Excel the task is reduced to a few clicks or taps followed by replication down a row or along a column, as discussed earlier.

For example, we could find the average amount spent on **Shopping** in a month and use this to predict the yearly expenditure.

Enter and center the labels **Average** and **£** in column **G** as shown below. Centering is discussed on page 48.

Click or tap the cell where the first average is to appear, cell **G5** in this example.

◢	A	B	C	D	E	F	G
1							
2							
3			Jan	Feb	Mar	Total	Average
4			£	£	£	£	£
5		Shopping	480.00	560.00	550.00	1590.00	
6		Petrol	170.00	165.00	180.00	515.00	
7		Heating	120.00	125.00	110.00	355.00	
8		Total	770.00	850.00	840.00	2460.00	
9							

Click or tap the **AutoSum** icon or, if necessary, the small arrow next to it, as shown on the right, to display the drop-down menu shown on the next page. (On iPads and iPhones select the **Formulas** tab on the ribbon and then tap **AutoSum** as shown on page 53).

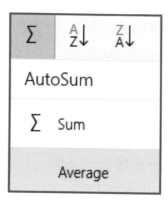

Then select **Average** from the menu, as shown above, to insert the formula into cell **G5** shown as shown below.

fx	=AVERAGE(C5:F5)						
	A	B	C	D	E	F	G	H
1								
2								
3			Jan	Feb	Mar	Total	Average	
4			£	£	£	£	£	
5		Shopping	480.00	560.00	550.00	1590.00	=AVERAGE(C5:F5)	
6		Petrol	170.00	165.00	180.00	515.00		

The Assumed Range is Wrong

This is because Excel assumes all of the cells in the row from **C5** to **F5** are to be added, incorrectly including the total, **1590**, in cell **F5**.

Correcting the Range

Drag the handles (the blue circles in the above example), to change the range to **C5** to **E5**. Alternatively click or tap in the formula bar and edit the formula shown above to:

=AVERAGE(C5:E5)

The corrected formula for the average is shown below in cell **G5**.

fx	=AVERAGE(C5:E5)						
◢	A	B	C	D	E	F	G	H
1								
2								
3			Jan	Feb	Mar	Total	Average	
4			£	£	£	£	£	
5		Shopping	480.00	560.00	550.00	1590.00	=AVERAGE(C5:E5)	
6		Petrol	170.00	165.00	180.00	515.00		
7		Heating	120.00	125.00	110.00	355.00		
8		Total	770.00	850.00	840.00	2460.00		
9								

Select the tick on the formula bar to insert the formula, making **G5** a *calculated cell*. Then only the *result*, **530** appears in the cell.

fx	=AVERAGE(C5:E5)					
◢	A	B	C	D	E	F	G
1							
2							
3			Jan	Feb	Mar	Total	Average
4			£	£	£	£	£
5		Shopping	480.00	560.00	550.00	1590.00	530.00
6		Petrol	170.00	165.00	180.00	515.00	
7		Heating	120.00	125.00	110.00	355.00	
8		Total	770.00	850.00	840.00	2460.00	
9							

Displaying Formulas

To display the formula used to produce a calculated cell, click or tap in the cell, such as **G5** above. The formula then appears in the formula bar, as shown above.

Now the averages can be completed down column **G** by replication as discussed on pages 44 to 46.

◢	A	B	C	D	E	F	G
1							
2							
3			Jan	Feb	Mar	Total	Average
4			£	£	£	£	£
5		Shopping	480.00	560.00	550.00	1590.00	530.00
6		Petrol	170.00	165.00	180.00	515.00	171.67
7		Heating	120.00	125.00	110.00	355.00	118.33
8		Total	770.00	850.00	840.00	2460.00	820.00
9							

Saving a Spreadsheet

Your Excel worksheets are automatically saved to the Internet cloud storage system, *Microsoft OneDrive*. This enables them to be *synced*, i.e. copied, to any other computers you may have. Copies of the files can also be downloaded and saved *locally* on your other computers, so they can be viewed, edited, etc., *offline* if necessary.

Automatic saving to OneDrive is switched on by default on tablets and phones, as shown on an iPad below.

The saving and syncing of Excel files using OneDrive is discussed in more detail in Chapter 9.

Summary: Creating a Spreadsheet

- The **AutoSum** feature is used to total rows and columns. **Average** produces typical middle values.

- Excel assumes a *range* of cells, which you can adjust if necessary by *dragging* on the worksheet or *editing* the formula in the formula bar.

- Click or tap the tick on the formula bar to *insert* the formula and produce a *calculated cell*.

- The calculated cell only displays the *result*. The formula is displayed in the formula bar.

- When you click or tap in a calculated cell at any time, the formula appears in the formula bar.

- A calculation can be *replicated* along a row or down a column by dragging or using the **FILL** option and *sliding* from the calculated cell. This automatically adjusts the cell references.

- To *select* an entire *row* or *column* of cells, click or tap in the row or column *header* cell.

- To select *multiple cells*, *drag* or *slide* across the required area. The selected cells are highlighted.

- Selected cells can be *formatted* and *edited* using icons on the ribbon, such as fonts, cell colours, number formats and insertion and deletion.

- Worksheet are automatically saved as *files* on *OneDrive Internet cloud storage*. Files can be *downloaded* for viewing off-line, if required.

Editing a Spreadsheet

Introduction

You need to save a permanent copy of a worksheet as a file so that in future it can be retrieved and opened for editing and updating with new information.

Fortunately, as discussed earlier, the latest versions of Excel have the **AutoSave** feature switched on by default. This automatically saves the file to OneDrive in the clouds. Then it can be opened on other computers you wish to use.

To open a spreadsheet saved in a previous session, start Excel as described on page 26. Your **Recent** files are listed in the left-hand panel. If you don't give a file a name, Excel assigns a default name such as **Book(1)**. Saving and naming files to OneDrive is discussed in more detail later.

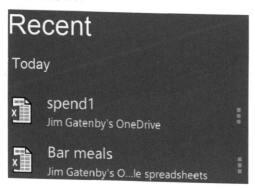

Click or tap the filename, such as **spend1** above, to open the worksheet as shown on the next page.

Inserting a New Column

For example, to insert a new column of spending for **April**, as shown below.

Right-click or tap and hold in the column header to the *right* of where the new column is to be inserted, in this case **F** shown below.

B	C	D	E	F	G
	Jan	Feb	Mar	Total	Average
	£	£	£	£	£
Shopping	480.00	560.00	550.00	1590.00	530.00

Then select **Insert** from the menu which pops up, as shown below. (The menus for Excel 2016 and the mobile versions of Excel are slightly different in their layout, but the essential options are the same).

✂	▤	⧉	∨	Clear	Fill	Insert	Delete	Hide

The new column is inserted to the left of the previously selected header, **F**, which now becomes column **G**, as shown below.

B	C	D	E	F	G	H
	Jan	Feb	Mar	April	Total	Average
	£	£	£	£	£	£
Shopping	480.00	560.00	550.00		1590.00	530.00

You can now enter the labels **April** and **£** and enter the numeric data for **April**, as shown below. The **Total** formula in **G5** should now be **=SUM(C5:F5)** to include **April**.

Replicate the formula **=SUM(C5:F5)** down column **G** by dragging or **FILL** and sliding as discussed on pages 44 to 46.

Should now be = SUM(C5:F5)

fx	=SUM(C5:E5)						
◢	A	B	C	D	E	F	G	H
1								
2								
3			Jan	Feb	Mar	April	Total	Average
4			£	£	£	£	£	£
5		Shopping	480.00	560.00	550.00	570.00	1590.00	530.00

Similarly the formula for **Average** in cell **H5** should be to be **=AVERAGE(C5:F5)**. The spreadsheet is shown below, with the **Total** and **Average** columns including the figures for **April**.

◢	A	B	C	D	E	F	G	H
1								
2								
3			Jan	Feb	Mar	April	Total	Average
4			£	£	£	£	£	£
5		Shopping	480.00	560.00	550.00	570.00	2160.00	540.00
6		Petrol	170.00	165.00	180.00	190.00	705.00	176.25
7		Heating	120.00	125.00	110.00	112.00	467.00	116.75
8		Total	770.00	850.00	840.00	872.00	3332.00	833.00
9								

Inserting a New Row

For example, to insert a new row in the previous spending spreadsheet to cover unexpected bills. The method is as follows:

Right-click or touch and hold the row header in the row *below* where the new row is to be inserted. **8** is the row header selected in this example, as shown below.

7		Heating	120.00	125.00	110.00	112.00	467.00	116.75
8		Total	770.00	850.00	840.00	872.00	3332.00	833.00
9								

Then select **Insert** from the pop-up menu, shown below.

A blank row is inserted as the new row **8**, while the **Total** row is now row **9**, as shown below.

7		Heating	120.00	125.00	110.00	112.00	467.00	116.75
8								
9		Total	770.00	850.00	840.00	872.00	3332.00	833.00

Enter the label **Bills** in row **8**, then enter the amounts spent in each column along row **8**, as shown below.

7		Heating	120.00	125.00	110.00	112.00	467.00	116.75
8		Bills	59.00	236.00	119.00	321.00	735.00	183.75
9		Total	829.00	1086.00	959.00	1193.00	4067.00	1016.75

You should see that the range in cell **C9** has automatically adjusted to take account of the new row **8** and should now be: **=SUM(C5:C8)**

After checking the formula in cell **C9** and then replicating this formula along row **9**, as discussed on pages 44-46, the amended sheet appears as shown below.

C9	▼	⋮	✕ ✓ ƒx		=SUM(C5:C8)			
◢	A	B	C	D	E	F	G	H
1								
2								
3			Jan	Feb	Mar	April	Total	Average
4			£	£	£	£	£	£
5		Shopping	480.00	560.00	550.00	570.00	2160.00	540.00
6		Petrol	170.00	165.00	180.00	190.00	705.00	176.25
7		Heating	120.00	125.00	110.00	112.00	467.00	116.75
8		Bills	59.00	236.00	119.00	321.00	735.00	183.75
9		Total	829.00	1086.00	959.00	1193.00	4067.00	1016.75
10								

Checking Cell References in Formulas

As shown on the previous pages, after inserting or deleting a row or column, the various versions of Excel usually adjust any formulas affected by the new cell references. For example, after inserting a new row, cell **C8** would become **C9**. However, in some circumstances, this automatic adjustment may not occur.

After inserting a row or column, it's a good idea to check that the cell ranges in any formulas are still correct.

Any incorrect ranges can be rectified by dragging on the worksheet using the circular handles on the blue rectangle (or similar), shown on page 43 or by editing the formula in the formula bar. Then replicate the corrected formula down the column or along a row, as discussed on page 44-46.

Updating and Automatic Recalculation

Suppose you find you've entered an incorrect amount, such as **321.00** in cell **F8** highlighted below.

f_x	=SUM(C5:C8)						
◢	A	B	C	D	E	F	G	H
1								
2								
3			Jan	Feb	Mar	April	Total	Average
4			£	£	£	£	£	£
5		Shopping	480.00	560.00	550.00	570.00	2160.00	540.00
6		Petrol	170.00	165.00	180.00	190.00	705.00	176.25
7		Heating	120.00	125.00	110.00	112.00	467.00	116.75
8		Bills	59.00	236.00	119.00	321.00	735.00	183.75
9		Total	829.00	1086.00	959.00	1793.00	4067.00	1016.75
10								

Incorrect entry

Double-click or double-tap in cell **F8**, then delete **321.00** and replace with the correct value, such as **219.00** in this particular example. Cell **F8** is used in the calculations for the **Total** in **G8**, **G9** and **F9** and the **Average** in **H8** and **H9**.

The *formulas* in these cells are still correct, since only the *data* in cell **F8** has changed with this correction. So Excel *automatically recalculates* cells **G8**, **H8** and **F9**, **G9** and **H9** as shown below.

Amended entry   New Total   New Average

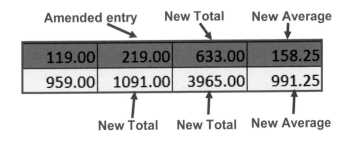

New Total   New Total   New Average

Multiplication

From the average monthly spending shown on the previous page you can easily calculate the likely annual spending, using the formula:

annual spending = average monthly spending*12

The asterisk (*) is the standard computer multiplication sign, replacing the traditional (**X**).

So we need to insert a new column **I** as shown below and discussed on page 58. Then insert new labels **Annual** and **£**.

F	G	H	I
April	Total	Average	Annual
£	£	£	£
570.00	2160.00	540.00	
190.00	705.00	176.25	
112.00	467.00	116.75	

To calculate the annual spending in cell **I5** we need to enter the formula **=H5*12** in cell **I5** as shown below.

=H5*12

E	F	G	H	I
Mar	April	Total	Average	Annual
£	£	£	£	£
550.00	570.00	2160.00	540.00	=H5*12
180.00	190.00	705.00	176.25	
110.00	112.00	467.00	116.75	

After selecting the tick in the formula bar, as discussed on page 31, the annual total for **Shopping**, **6480**, appears in cell **I5** as shown below.

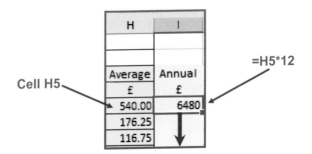

The formula **=H5*12** can easily be *replicated*, as discussed on pages 44-46, by dragging or swiping down column **I**, as indicated by the red arrow above. This produces the **Annual** spending figures in cells **I6** to **I9** as shown below.

I9		▼	⋮	✕ ✓	f_x	=H9*12		
	A	B	C	D	E	F	G	H	I
1									
2									
3			Jan	Feb	Mar	April	Total	Average	Annual
4			£	£	£	£	£	£	£
5		Shopping	480.00	560.00	550.00	570.00	2160.00	540.00	6480.00
6		Petrol	170.00	165.00	180.00	190.00	705.00	176.25	2115.00
7		Heating	120.00	125.00	110.00	112.00	467.00	116.75	1401.00
8		Bills	59.00	236.00	119.00	219.00	633.00	158.25	1899.00
9		Total	829.00	1086.00	959.00	1091.00	3965.00	991.25	11895.00
10									

All the *formulas*, rather than the *results* of the calculations replicated down the **Annual** column **I** are shown on page 69, together with the formulas for **Total** and **Average**.

Division

The weekly spending can be found using the formula:

weekly spending = annual spending/52

The forward slash (/) is the standard computing sign for division, replacing the traditional (÷).

So we need to insert a new column **J** and the labels **Weekly** and **£**. Then enter the formula **=I5/52** in cell **J5**, as shown below.

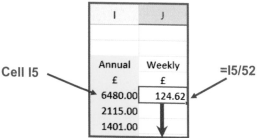

Finally the formula is replicated down column **J**, as discussed on pages 44-46, to produce the **Weekly** figures shown below.

J9			fx	=I9/52						
	A	B	C	D	E	F	G	H	I	J
1										
2										
3			Jan	Feb	Mar	April	Total	Average	Annual	Weekly
4			£	£	£	£	£	£	£	£
5		Shopping	480.00	560.00	550.00	570.00	2160.00	540.00	6480.00	124.62
6		Petrol	170.00	165.00	180.00	190.00	705.00	176.25	2115.00	40.67
7		Heating	120.00	125.00	110.00	112.00	467.00	116.75	1401.00	26.94
8		Bills	59.00	236.00	119.00	219.00	633.00	158.25	1899.00	36.52
9		Total	829.00	1086.00	959.00	1091.00	3965.00	991.25	11895.00	228.75
10										

What If?

Suppose prices in general were forecast to rise by 7%, for example. To increase the **Weekly** spending by 7% we multiply by a *scale factor* of **1.07**. So the formula **=J5*1.07** is inserted in cell **K5** as shown below on the left. If you're a bit rusty on percentages, a few examples are given at the bottom of the page.

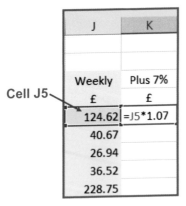

Cell J5

After clicking or tapping the tick in the formula bar to insert the formula, the calculation is then replicated down column **K** as discussed on pages 44-46 and shown above on the right. Some common percentages and the corresponding scale factors to multiply by are shown below.

% Increase	Scale Factor
5%	1.05
15%	1.15
25%	1.25
50%	1.50
100%	2.00

% decrease	Scale Factor
5%	0.95
15%	0.85
25%	0.75
50%	0.50
100%	0.00

VAT

Value Added Tax is a government levy added to the sales price of various items. The rates are decided by the Chancellor of the Exchequer. VAT is paid by the customer to the seller of goods or services, who then passes it on to the government.

Currently there are three rates of VAT:

Standard rate: 20% (previously 17.5%)

Charged on most goods and services.

Reduced rate: 5%

E.g. Domestic fuel, energy saving products, children's car seats.

Zero rate: 0%

E.g. Food, children's clothes, books.

So, for example, to calculate the VAT-inclusive price on standard rate items, i.e. 20%, we multiply the basic price or VAT-exclusive price by 1.20.

Similarly to find the VAT-inclusive price at the reduced rate, i.e. 5%, we multiply by 1.05.

This would be done by *replication*, as shown on the previous page when multiplying by 1.07 to increase an amount by 7%.

To calculate the VAT-exclusive price from the VAT-inclusive price, you would divide by 1.20 for the standard rate and divide by 1.05 at the reduced rate.

Itemising the VAT

If you need to show the VAT separately, use the formulas:

VAT at 20% (Standard rate):

VAT= Basic price * 0.20

VAT at 5% (Reduced rate):

VAT=Basic price * 0.05

Also: **Total price = Basic price +VAT.**

So, for example, a car repair bill might be worked out on a spreadsheet, with VAT at 20%.

fx	= B3 + C3		
◢	A	B	C	D
1				
2	Item	Basic price	VAT (20%)	Total price (inc.VAT)
3	Clutch assembly	126.13	25.23	= B3 + C3
4	Brake Discs	55.98	11.20	
5	Brake pads	27.32	5.46	=B3*0.20
6	Labour	210.00	42.00	
7	Total	419.43	83.89	

=**B3*0.20** is replicated down column **C**.

=**B3+C3** is replicated down column **D**.

fx	= B7 + C7		
◢	A	B	C	D
1				
2	Item	Basic price	VAT (20%)	Total price (inc.VAT)
3	Clutch assembly	126.13	25.23	151.36
4	Brake Discs	55.98	11.20	67.18
5	Brake pads	27.32	5.46	32.78
6	Labour	210.00	42.00	252.00
7	Total	419.43	83.89	503.32

=**B3+C3**

Displaying Formulas in All Calculated Cells

Shown below is a section of the earlier spending spreadsheet. Normally the calculated cells only display the *results* of the calculation, not the *formula* itself. In Excel 2016, you can switch on the display of all of the formulas in a worksheet, as shown below. From the **File** menu on the ribbon, select **Options** and **Advanced** then scroll down and tick the check box shown below.

☑ Show formulas in cells instead of their calculated results

G	H	I	J	K
Total	Average	Annual	Weekly	Plus 7%
£	£	£	£	£
=SUM(C5:F5)	=AVERAGE(C5:F5)	=H5*12	=I5/52	=J5*1.07
=SUM(C6:F6)	=AVERAGE(C6:F6)	=H6*12	=I6/52	=J6*1.07
=SUM(C7:F7)	=AVERAGE(C7:F7)	=H7*12	=I7/52	=J7*1.07
=SUM(C8:F8)	=AVERAGE(C8:F8)	=H8*12	=I8/52	=J8*1.07
=SUM(C9:F9)	=AVERAGE(C9:F9)	=H9*12	=I9/52	=J9*1.07

Displaying a Formula in a Single Cell

As discussed earlier, you can display the formula in an individual cell in all versions of Excel by clicking or tapping the cell. The formula is displayed in the formula bar as shown below.

fx	=SUM(C5:F5)					
◢	A	B	C	D	E	F	G
1							
2							
3			Jan	Feb	Mar	April	Total
4			£	£	£	£	£
5		Shopping	480.00	560.00	550.00	570.00	2160.00

Summary: Editing a Spreadsheet

- New columns can be inserted, to the *left* of a selected column. Column cell references are adjusted accordingly.

- New rows are inserted *above* a selected row. Row cell references are adjusted accordingly.

- Cell references in formulas in calculated cells are normally adjusted automatically but this should be checked after new rows or columns are inserted.

- When you amend the numbers in a data cell, Excel *automatically recalculates* all of the affected calculated cells in the worksheet.

- Excel uses the standard computer signs (*) and (/) for the mathematical operations of *multiplication* and *division* respectively.

- To *increase* a row or column of numbers by a percentage, e.g. 17%, multiply by a scale factor, in this case 1.17, using *replication* down a column or along a row, as discussed on pages 44-46.

- Similarly to decrease a row or column of numbers by a percentage, e.g. 25%, multiply by a *scale factor*, in this case 0.75.

- Excel 2016 allows you to display the formulas in all the calculated cells, using the **File/Options/Advanced** menu on the ribbon.

- Click or tap a single calculated cell to display its formula in the formula bar as shown on page 69.

Pop-up Menus

Introduction

Many of the major tasks in Excel are accessed from the *ribbon* across the top of a worksheet. These include the **File** menu with options such as **New**, **Open**, **Save** and **Print**.

In contrast, *context sensitive menus* do not appear on the ribbon but "pop up" on the screen to provide options which are relevant to your current cursor position. Context sensitive menus appear in all versions of Excel when you:

- Right-click or tap in a *column* or *row header*.
- Right-click or tap and hold then release in a *cell*.
- Right-click in a selected group of cells.
- Select a group of cells using touch as discussed on page 47 — then the menu pops up automatically.

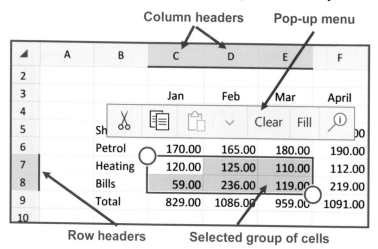

Menu options displayed after right-clicking or tapping in a column or row header apply to all of the cells in the column or row.

The following menus are displayed after right-clicking or tapping in a *column header*. Menus displayed after right-clicking or tapping in the *row headers* are basically the same.

Header Menus: Excel 2016 and Excel Mobile

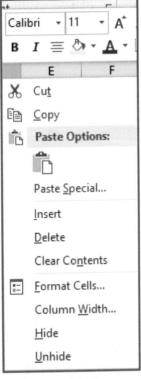

Excel 2016   **Excel Mobile**

Excel for Android Header Menus

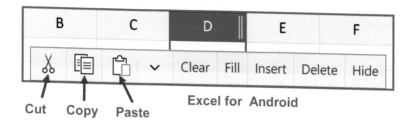

Cut   Copy   Paste   **Excel for Android**

Tapping the small arrow shown on the right and above on the Excel for Android menu opens the **Paste** menu, with additional options relative to the basic **Paste** icon shown above.

Paste Options

First select a cell then copy the contents using the **Copy** icon shown above. A cell may simply contain a numerical *value*, e.g. **27**, or it may be a *calculated cell* with both a *formula* and a *value* or *result*. Or the cell may have some *formatting* such as a border, a fill colour or a certain font, or style of lettering, for example. The menu shown on the right allows you to select which properties of a copied cell you wish to paste to a new cell.

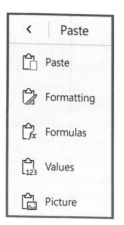

Fill

This command is discussed on page 45 and 81. This allows you to copy a cell or group of cells by dragging into adjacent cells, including replicating a formula along a row or down a column.

Excel for iOS (iPad and iPhone) Header Menus

When you tap in a *column header* on an iPad or iPhone, the menu shown below appears.

Cut	Copy	Paste	Insert Left	Delete	Clear

Insert Left inserts a new column on the left of the currently selected column.

If you tap in a *row header* on the iPad and iPhone, a slightly different menu appears, as shown below.

Cut	Copy	Paste	Clear	Insert Above	Delete

Insert Above inserts a new row above the currently selected row.

Working with Rows and Columns
(Applies to All Versions of Excel)

The menus on pages 72, 73 and on this page above were displayed after right-clicking or tapping in the column or row headers. Although the Excel 2016 menu is more complex than the mobile versions, they all have the same basic options such as to **Cut**, **Copy**, **Paste**, **Clear**, **Insert** and **Delete** rows and columns. These can be used to add, remove, move or duplicate rows and columns, As discussed shortly, similar menus and options can be displayed from selected cells and from selected groups of cells.

Other menu options such as **Fill** and **Hide** shown on pages 72 and 73 are discussed elsewhere in this chapter.

Inserting a Column

Insert or **Insert Left** inserts a blank column to the *left* of the currently selected column. For example, cell contents previously in column **D** will now be in column **E**.

Inserting a Row

Insert or **Insert Above** inserts a blank row *above* the currently selected row. For example, cell contents previously in row **7** will now be in row **8**.

Deleting a Column

Delete removes a selected column. So, for example, deleting column **E** will cause the original column **F** to become the new column **E**.

Deleting a Row

Delete removes a selected row. So, for example deleting row **6** would cause the original row **7** to become the new row **6**.

Fortunately the **Undo** and **Redo** icons shown on the right and on page 42 allow you to quickly correct any mistakes, including undoing a series of several actions.

Clearing versus Deleting

Clearing a column or row removes the contents from the row or column and leaves the row or header references the same. So, for example, after clearing a column in a 5 column worksheet, there will still be 5 columns, including the newly blank one.

Deleting a column from a 5 column worksheet, for example, will produce a 4 column worksheet and the column header references will be adjusted accordingly.

Selecting Multiple Rows and Columns

With a mouse, click and hold in the centre of a row or column header then drag down the row headers or along the column headers to select all of the required rows or columns.

With a touch screen, tap to select a row header then touch and drag one of the two circles which appear, as shown below, for selecting multiple rows.

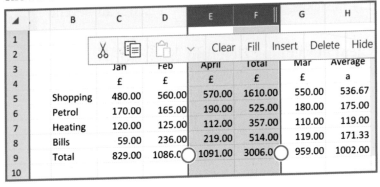

◢	A	B	C	D	E	F	G	H
1								
2			✂	📋	🗒 ⌄	Clear	Fill	Insert	Delete
3								
4			£	£	£	£	£	£
5		Shopping	480.00	560.00	550.00	57?00	2160.00	540.00
6		Petrol	170.00	165.00	180.00	?0.00	705.00	176.25
7		Heating	120.00	125.00	110.00	112.00	467.00	116.75
8		Total	770.00	850.00	?40.00	87?00	3332.00	833.00
9								

Drag a circle to select multiple rows

The same method is used for selecting multiple columns, as shown below.

◢	B	C	D	E	F	G	H
1							
2		✂ 📋 🗒 ⌄		Clear	Fill	Insert	Delete	Hide
3		Jan	Feb	April	Total	Mar	Average
4		£	£	£	£	£	a
5	Shopping	480.00	560.00	570.00	1610.00	550.00	536.67
6	Petrol	170.00	165.00	190.00	525.00	180.00	175.00
7	Heating	120.00	125.00	112.00	357.00	110.00	119.00
8	Bills	59.00	236.00	219.00	514.00	119.00	171.33
9	Total	829.00	1086.0	1091.00	3006.0	959.00	1002.00
10							

Hiding Rows and Columns

All of the versions of Excel have a **Hide** option on the menus obtained by right-clicking or tapping in a row or column header. These menus, including the **Hide** option, are shown on pages 72 and 73 for PC and Android devices. On iOS (iPads and iPhones), the **Hide** option, shown below, is located on the right of the header menus.

Insert Left	Delete	Clear	Hide	AutoFit

Column header menu: iPads and iPhones

The following example is based on an Android tablet, but the same general method applies to all of the platforms, PC, Android, iOS (iPad and iPhone, etc.)

To hide the **Total** column shown below, right-click or tap in the column header, **G**, then select **Hide** from the menu.

Hide selected column

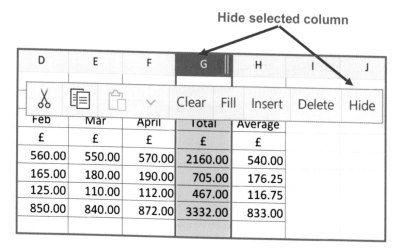

After clicking or tapping **Hide** as shown on the previous page, the **Total** column **G** disappears completely, including the column header **G**, as shown below.

Total column G now hidden

B	C	D	E	F	H
	Jan	Feb	Mar	April	Average
	£	£	£	£	£
Shopping	480.00	560.00	550.00	570.00	540.00
Petrol	170.00	165.00	180.00	190.00	176.25
Heating	120.00	125.00	110.00	112.00	116.75

Unhiding Rows and Columns

Select the two columns (or rows), either side of the hidden column or row. In the above example this is columns **F** and **H** as shown selected below. (Selecting multiple rows and columns is discussed on page 76). Now select **Unhide** from the menu shown below, which appears automatically.

C	D	E	F	H	I	J	K

| ✂ | ▤ | 📋 | ⌄ | Clear | Fill | Insert | Delete | Hide | Unhide |

£	£	£	£	£	
480.00	560.00	550.00	570.00	540.00	
170.00	165.00	180.00	190.00	176.25	
120.00	125.00	110.00	112.00	116.75	

This causes the **Total** column **G** to be restored to the screen, as shown on page 77.

Pop-up Menus from Selected Cells

The notes on this page apply to single cells and groups of cells, (but not to entire rows and columns, just discussed). To select a single cell, click or tap, hold and release in the cell. To select a group of cells, with a mouse, drag over the required area. With a touch screen, tap one of the cells then slide one of the handles which appear, as shown on the right, to highlight the required group of cells.

Excel 2016

When you right-click in a selected cell or group of selected cells in Excel 2016, the menu below is displayed

Mobile Versions of Excel

Right-click or tap, hold and release in a single cell. When you select a group of cells on mobile devices, the top two menus shown below are displayed automatically. With a mouse right-click in the selected group of cells.

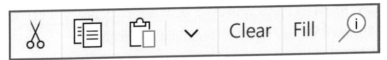

Excel for Android

Excel for iOS (iPad and iPhone)

Excel Mobile

These cell-based menus on page 80 are simpler than the header-based menus on pages, 72-74, which apply to entire rows and columns. Unlike rows and columns, you cannot **Insert** or **Delete** single cells or groups of cells. You can, however, **Clear** or wipe the *contents* of a single cell or a group of cells. You can also use **Cut** and **Paste** and **Copy** and **Paste** to either *duplicate* or *move* contents of a cell or group of cells to another part of a worksheet.

Wrap

The **Wrap** command on the iOS menu on page 80 increases the row height if the contents of a cell are too large to be fully displayed, as shown below.

Fill

The **Fill** command on all of the menus page 80 is used to copy a cell or group of cells to adjacent cells on the worksheet. Select **Fill** in the current cell or group of cells. Then drag a handle as shown on the left below.

In this example, Excel automatically adjusts the week numbers as shown above.

Fill is also used to *replicate* a formula along a row or down a column, automatically adjusting any cell ranges in the formula, as discussed on page 45.

In Excel 2016, the replication is achieved by dragging the plus sign (+) in the bottom right-hand corner of a cell.

Changing the Column Width and Row Height

With a mouse, hover the cursor at the edge of the column or row headers. Then drag the + sign as shown below left.

With a touch screen, tap the row or column header, then drag or slide the two small vertical parallel lines.

Mouse   **Touch screen**

Summary: Pop-up Menus

- Although the pop-up menus on the mobile versions of Excel are simpler than those on Excel 2016, the essential tools such as **Cut, Copy, Paste, Insert, Delete, Clear** and **Hide** are all present.

- Worksheets created in Excel 2016 can be imported into the mobile versions and edited, but some more advanced formatting features may not be shown.

- Menus applicable to rows and columns are displayed by *right-clicking* or *tapping* in the row or column *header*.

- Menus applicable to single cells are displayed after *right-clicking* or *tapping*, *holding* and *releasing* in the selected cell. With touch, when you drag to select a group cells, menus pop up automatically.

- The **FILL** option makes it easy to copy cells and groups of cells, including automatic adjustments to any labels such as **week1, week2**, etc.

Graphs and Charts

Introduction

Graphs and charts allow numbers to be analysed and compared at a glance; trends can be spotted and predictions made about the way things may develop in the future. Drawing graphs and charts by hand can be quite a difficult and time-consuming process; programs like Excel reduce the drawing of all sorts of graphs to a quick and simple operation involving a few clicks with a mouse or taps with a finger. The basic method is as follows:

- The data to be used in the graph or chart is entered into an Excel spreadsheet.
- The numbers and labels to be "plotted" are selected i.e. highlighted in the rows or columns.
- The type of graph or chart required is selected from the wide choice available on the Excel ribbon; for example, pie chart, column chart and line graph.
- Excel works out the scales for any horizontal and vertical axes and immediately draws the graph.
- Headings, etc., can be added easily and the graph or chart is saved as part of the spreadsheet.
- The graph or chart can be printed separately.
- The graph or chart can be inserted into a report or other document in a word processor.

Types of Chart

The Pie Chart

Garden Birds

The pie chart shows how different items in varying quantities contribute to a total. Various options are available to label the slices of the pie, including displaying the name of each item in the slice and the percentage of the total.

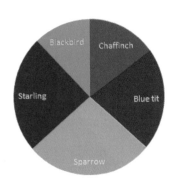

The Line Graph

The line graph shows how a quantity varies over a period of time. The time in weeks, months or years, for example is normally plotted along the horizontal scale with the quantity being plotted on the vertical scale.

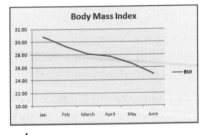

The Column Chart

This chart is useful for comparing quantities side by side; for example to compare the total weekly sales of different bar meals. You can alter the range of the scales and edit and format the titles, labels and text and background colours.

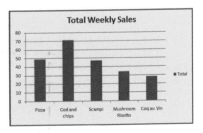

Drawing a Pie Chart

The data for this simple pie chart is entered into Excel as shown below.

	A	B
1	Garden Birds	
2	Bird	Number
3	Chaffinch	5
4	Blue tit	7
5	Sparrow	9
6	Starling	8
7	Blackbird	7

You can apply some colours to the text and backgrounds as discussed in the last chapter. Or select a different font from the Excel ribbon with the **Home** tab selected.

Now drag from cell **A3** to cell **B7**, as discussed on page 47 so that all of the data is highlighted, as shown below. Do not include the titles in the selection area at this stage – they can be added later.

	A	B
1	Garden Birds	
2	Bird	Number
3	Chaffinch	5
4	Blue tit	7
5	Sparrow	9
6	Starling	8
7	Blackbird	7

Selected data

Now select the **Insert** tab on the ribbon. Excel 2016 has icons for the various chart types displayed on the ribbon itself, as shown below.

Insert

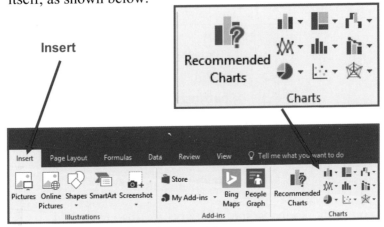

On the mobile versions of Excel you need to select the **Insert** tab on the ribbon, then select **Chart** or **Charts** as shown below.

Android Excel ribbon

iPad or iPhone Excel ribbon

Selecting the **Chart(s)** group displays icons for the various types of graph and chart such as **Column**, **Line**, **Pie** and **Bar**. The screenshot below is based on Excel for iOS (iPad and iPhone), but the options are the same for all versions of Excel.

Choosing a chart type

If you select **Recommended** shown above, Excel suggests various chart types to display your selected data. (On a tablet or phone you may need to rotate the screen into *landscape mode* to see the **Recommended** icon on the ribbon).

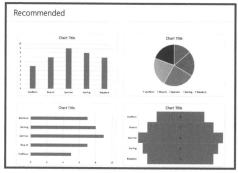

Excel recommended chart types

If you select the **Pie** icon as shown under **Charts** on the previous page, you can choose from several types of pie chart such as the two shown below.

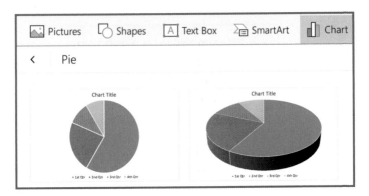

Click the type of pie chart you want and it instantly appears, embedded in the spreadsheet, as shown below.

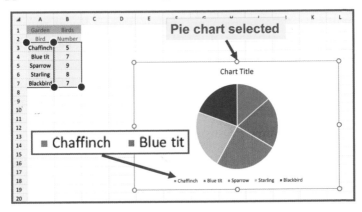

Below the pie chart shown above, Excel has included a *key* to the colours used in the slices of the pie, as shown below.

■ Chaffinch   ■ Blue tit   ■ Sparrow   ■ Starling   ■ Blackbird

Pie Chart Styles

Excel 2016

Select or highlight the pie chart by tapping or clicking. Selection is indicated by small circles around the rectangular frame, as shown on the previous page.

On Excel 2016, having selected a chart, as discussed on page 87 and shown on page 88, two new tabs, **Design** and **Format** pop up under **Chart Tools** on the ribbon, as shown on the right and below. The various chart styles appear in a row on the ribbon on Excel 2016. There is a scroll bar to display more styles.

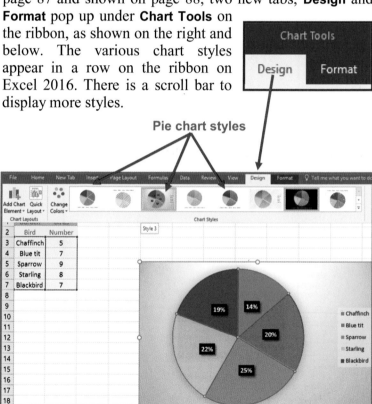

Pie chart styles

Pie Chart Styles

Mobile Versions of Excel

On mobile versions of Excel, when you select or highlight the pie chart as shown on page 88, the **Chart** tab pops up as shown below. Click or tap the **Chart** tab and then select **Style** to view and choose one of the available styles.

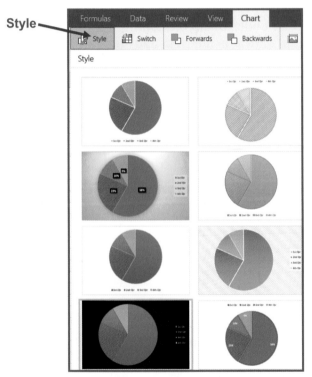

Pie chart styles on mobile versions of Excel

Having selected a **Chart Style**, the amended pie chart appears on the worksheet as shown on the next page. The pie chart styles are very similar on all versions of Excel.

Changing the Layout

Excel 2016

The **Quick Layout** feature in the **Chart Layouts** group on the **Design** tab presents various options as shown below.

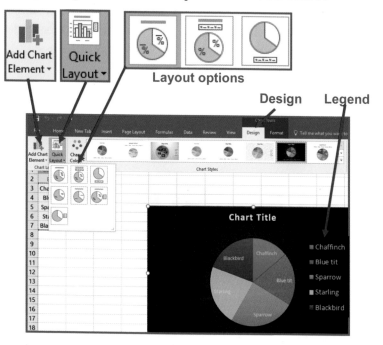

Options on the **Quick Layout** menu include the labelling of each slice as a percentage or with the name of each type of bird. You can also hide or display the *legend* or key as shown on the right above. The legend can be placed in various positions and these options are shown in full when you select **Add Chart Element** and **Legend** from the **Chart Layouts** group on the ribbon. You can also add your own title, such as **Garden Birds**, by editing in the **Chart Title** box.

Changing the Layout

Mobile Versions of Excel

Select the pie chart by clicking or tapping, indicated by the small circles on the rectangle as shown on page 88. Then select **Layout** from the **Chart** tab, as shown below. A range of layouts is displayed, as shown by the small sample below. The **Layout** options are similar to those for Excel 2016, described at the bottom of page 91.

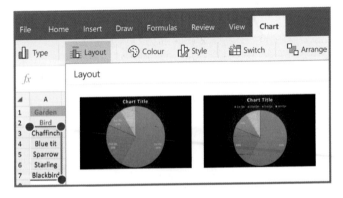

A sample layout, including a title, legend and % labels on the slices is shown below.

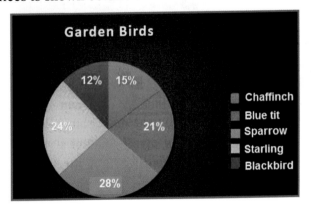

Updating a Pie Chart

When a graph or chart is embedded in a spreadsheet as shown below, there is a live link between the data in the cells of the worksheet and the chart. If you make a change to the numerical data or a label in the spreadsheet, the graph or chart is automatically redrawn to reflect the new data or label.

In the garden bird example, the number for the **Blackbird** in cell **B7** is increased to **11**. The pie chart is automatically adjusted to show the new slices with the **Blackbird** slice increased to **28%** from **12%** as shown on the previous page. The increase in the number of blackbirds also results in a corresponding automatic decrease in the size of the slices and percentages for the other birds.

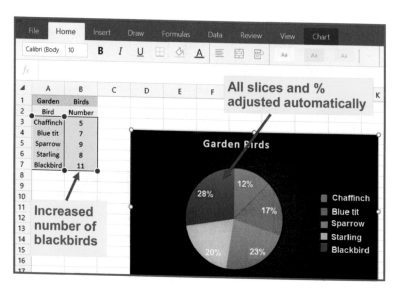

The Line Graph

The line graph is usually plotted along horizontal and vertical scales, known as the *X* and *Y axes*. The horizontal scale is often used to show the passing of time in weeks, months, days or years, for example. The vertical scale is used to plot the *variable* or quantity changing over a period of time. Points are plotted at each point in time and the points joined up to form the line graph, as shown below.

Working out the scales for the x and y axes can be quite a difficult job but Excel does this automatically for you.

When you tap or right-click to select a graph or chart on a worksheet, a menu pops up with options to **Cut, Copy** or **Delete** the graph or chart. For example, to copy the graph or chart and paste it into a document or report.

Monitoring Body Mass Index

The spreadsheet below shows a person's weight as they follow a dieting program for six months from January to June. Body Mass Index (BMI) is a measure of a person's weight in relation to their height; a BMI above certain limits suggests that a person may be classified as obese. The formula used to calculate BMI is as follows:

$$\text{BMI} = \frac{\textbf{Weight in Kilograms}}{\textbf{(Height in Metres) x (Height in Metres)}}$$

The **Height** squared i.e. multiplied by itself, is obtained by entering the formula **=C4*C4** in cell **D4**. This is replicated down column **D** by dragging the small cross from the corner of cell **D4**.

	A	B	C	D	E
1			Body Mass Index (BMI)		
2					
3	Month	Weight kg	Height (M)	Height Squared (M^2)	BMI
4	Jan	79	1.6	2.56	30.86
5	Feb	75	1.6	2.56	29.30
6	March	72	1.6	2.56	28.13
7	April	71	1.6	2.56	27.73
8	May	68	1.6	2.56	26.56
9	June	64	1.6	2.56	25.00

The **BMI** is then calculated in cell **E4** by entering the formula **=B4/D4**. Then the remaining **BMI** values are calculated by replicating from cell **E4** down cells **E5** to **E9**. as discussed on pages 44-46.

We could miss out column **C** and **D** and simply enter the formula **=B4/(1.6*1.6)** in cell **C4** since this person's height will always be **1.6** metres. However, the method in the above worksheet is more explicit and can easily be adapted for people of different heights.

The problem now is to plot a line graph showing the months on the horizontal scale and the **BMI** on the vertical scale. To do this we first need to select or highlight the data in columns **A** and **E** only. This can't be done by simply dragging over **Column A** followed by **Column E,** since clicking and dragging in **Column E** deselects **Column A**.

Selecting Cells in Two Non-adjacent Columns

Excel 2016: Mouse Operation

This is done, in this example, by dragging the cursor down over cells **A3-A9**. Then holding down the **Ctrl** key and dragging over cells **E3-E9**. The extract below shows the **BMI** worksheet with the data and column headings in columns **A** and **E** highlighted and ready to be plotted.

Selected cells

	A	B	C	D	E
1			Body Mass Index (BMI)		
2					
3	Month	Weight kg	Height (M)	Height Squared (M^2)	BMI
4	Jan	79	1.6	2.56	30.86
5	Feb	75	1.6	2.56	29.30
6	March	72	1.6	2.56	28.13
7	April	71	1.6	2.56	27.73
8	May	68	1.6	2.56	26.56
9	June	64	1.6	2.56	25.00
10					

Moving Two Non-adjacent Columns Together

Mobile Versions of Excel (Android and iOS)

Two non-adjacent columns can be placed together by selecting the relevant cells in one column by dragging the circles as shown on the right. Then *copy and paste* the cells into the required position as discussed in Chapters 5 and 6. On iOS (iPad and iPhone) the selected cells can also be *dragged* into the new position.

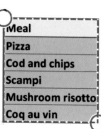

Then the two columns can be selected as shown below.

In the example below, a blank column was inserted to the left of the old column **E**, then column **A** was copied and pasted to become the new column **E**. Before pasting select the required empty cells in the new column by dragging the circles.

	D	E	F
	Height squared	Month	BMI
	2.56	Jan	30.86
	2.56	Feb	29.30
	2.56	Mar	28.13
	2.56	Apr	27.73
	2.56	May	26.56
	2.56	Jun	25.00

Column A copied into newly inserted column E

Now it's just a case of dragging over the new columns **E** and **F,** ready to select and format the type of graph required.

Drawing the Line Graph

As with the pie chart on pages 86 and 87, for mobile versions of Excel select **Chart** and then **Line**. For Excel 2016 select the line graph icon on the ribbon as shown on page 86. Several formats for line graphs are displayed as shown in the small sample below.

Select one of the line graph formats and the selected columns on the worksheet are immediately displayed on the worksheet as a line graph as shown below.

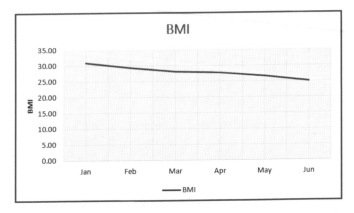

As discussed earlier in this chapter in the pie chart section, with the line graph selected on the worksheet there are options for changing the style, colours and layout of the line graph. This is done using the **Chart** or **Charts** tab on mobile versions of Excel and the **Design** tab on Excel 2016.

Several Lines on One Chart

The small worksheet below shows average daily high temperatures for three holiday destinations. To compare all three resorts on a single line graph, select, i.e. highlight all of the data including the months, the resort names and the temperatures as shown below. (Selecting groups or blocks of cells is discussed on page 47). Then select a line graph type as discussed on page 98.

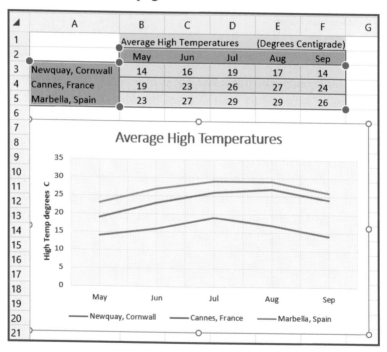

Excel automatically assigns a different colour to each resort and plots them as separate line graphs. After selecting the chart as indicated by the small circles above, you can change the style and layout of the chart and add a title as shown above and discussed in the earlier pie chart section.

Drawing a Column Chart

This chart will be based on the **Bar Meals** spreadsheet shown below.

▲	A	B	C	D	E	F	G
1				Bar Meals			
2	Meal	Tues	Wed	Thu	Fri	Sat	Total
3	Pizza	3	8	9	12	17	49
4	Cod and chips	7	6	14	23	21	71
5	Scampi	2	6	8	13	18	47
6	Mushroom risotto	3	6	5	8	12	34
7	Coq au vin	0	8	4	7	9	28
8	Total	15	34	40	63	77	229

A column chart for the sales **Total** in a week for each meal will make it easier to see the most popular dishes. We need to select the **Meal** column **A**, and the **Total** column **G**.

As mentioned on pages 96 and 97, in Excel 2016 using a mouse, selecting cells in two non-adjacent columns can be achieved with a mouse by dragging over the required cells in the first column. Then, while holding down the **Ctrl** key, dragging over the required cells in the second column. You don't need to select the labels, such as **Meal** — these can be added later if necessary. In this example cells **A3** to **A7** and **G3** to **G7** were selected, as shown in blue below.

Selected cells

▲	A	B	C	D	E	F	G
1				Bar Meals			
2	Meal	Tues	Wed	Thu	Fri	Sat	Total
3	Pizza	3	8	9	12	17	49
4	Cod and chips	7	6	14	23	21	71
5	Scampi	2	6	8	13	18	47
6	Mushroom risotto	3	6	5	8	12	34
7	Coq au vin	0	8	4	7	9	28
8	Total	15	34	40	63	77	229

On mobile versions of Excel using a touch screen, you can move two non-adjacent columns together by *copying* and *pasting*, as discussed on page 98 and in Chapters 5 and 6.

G	H
Meal	**Total**
Pizza	49
Cod and chips	71
Scampi	47
Mushroom risotto	34
Coq au vin	28
Total	229

Now the **Meal** and **Total** columns are adjacent, the relevant cells, **G3** to **G7** and **H3** to **H7** can be selected as shown above in blue. Then they can be used to create the column chart.

Now on Excel 2016 select **Insert** and then select the **Column Chart** icon on the ribbon. On mobile versions of Excel, select the **Insert** tab, then the **Chart** tab and **Column**.

A choice of column chart types is then displayed as shown in the example below from Excel 2016.

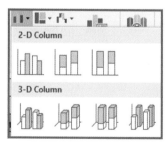

After you click on a column chart design, the chart immediately appears on the worksheet. You can then use the Excel **Layout** and **Style** features, discussed earlier in this chapter, to change the colours and add labels to the axes and a **Chart Title**, etc., as shown below.

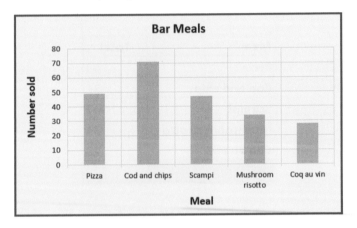

Drawing a Clustered Column Chart

This chart will show the sales of each meal side by side on the different nights. It is drawn after selecting all of the meals for every day. This can be achieved by dragging diagonally from cell **A2** to cell **F7** as shown in green in the example below.

◢	A	B	C	D	E	F	G
1				Bar Meals			
2	Meal	Tues	Wed	Thu	Fri	Sat	Total
3	Pizza	3	8	9	12	17	49
4	Cod and chips	7	6	14	23	21	71
5	Scampi	2	6	8	13	18	47
6	Mushroom risotto	3	6	5	8	12	34
7	Coq au vin	0	8	4	7	9	28
8	Total		15	34	40	63	77	229
9							

To draw the clustered column graph first select the Insert tab on the ribbon, then **Chart** and select **Column**. A selection of column charts is displayed including the **Clustered Column chart** shown on the left below.

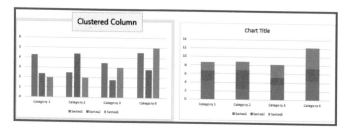

When you select this icon the clustered column graph appears, as shown below.

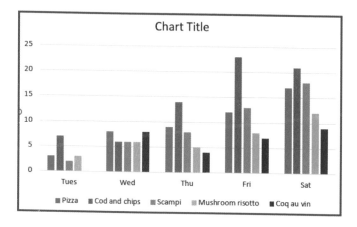

In drawing the above clustered column chart, very little input is required from the user. It's simply a case of entering the data into the worksheet, selecting the required cells and then choosing and selecting the clustered column format. Excel arranges the layout, the colours and the legend automatically as shown above.

Summary: Graphs and Charts

- Excel makes the relatively complex task of drawing graphs and chart into a very easy one.

- Simply enter the data and select the required labels and numbers, then choose a chart/graph type.

- Cells in two non-adjacent columns can be selected for plotting by holding down the **CTRL** key (mouse and keyboard). With a touch screen use *copy* and *paste* to make the two columns adjacent.

- Excel has an option to *recommend* alternative chart types for the data selected on the worksheet.

- Excel automatically creates a **Legend** or key to identify the data displayed on a graph or chart.

- The **Style** and **Layout** options allow variations in the display of labels, percentages, a chart title, the **Legend** and colour schemes.

- When you change a number in the worksheet data the graph or chart is *updated* automatically.

- A graph or chart is embedded in a worksheet and saved with the worksheet as a single .**xlsx** file.

- Worksheets and charts can be created in any of the versions of Excel and transferred between them.

- The basic methods for creating and formatting graphs and charts are the same for Excel 2016 and all of the mobile versions of Excel.

Using Excel for Text

Introduction

The main use of spreadsheets is to automate calculations on large tables of figures and enable charts and graphs to be drawn easily. However, the layout of the spreadsheet in organized rows and columns makes it very easy to enter and create a simple *database* such as a file of names and addresses. Once entered and saved in Excel, the names and addresses can easily be *updated* by amending details or adding new people. Excel also allows the *sorting* of records into order and the *filtering* of records containing particular information. This might for example, be useful to:

- The secretary of a club, group or society keeping membership details and sending out regular newsletters.

- A business sending out invoices, special offers, etc., to customers and clients.

- An organization wishing to keep personal details of staff or students, etc.

- Anyone sending out a lot of invitations, greetings or Christmas cards, etc.

- The use of Excel as a *data source* for inserting names and addresses in standard letters and printing address labels is discussed in Chapter 12.

As discussed in Chapter 12, an Excel name and address file may be used as the *data source* for importing a large number of names and addresses into a *mail merge* program in a word processor such as Microsoft Word 2016. This allows address labels to be printed very quickly, saving a great deal of time compared with manual methods.

Creating an Address File in Excel

Open a new, blank worksheet as discussed on page 26. Then start entering the column headings, such as **First Name**, **Surname**, **Address Line 1**, **Address Line 2**, etc., as shown in the extract below. These play an important part in the mail merge, as discussed in Chapter 12.

You'll probably need to extend the width of the columns to accommodate the column headings and also the data. Changing the width of columns by dragging in the column headers was discussed on page 82 and is shown again below.

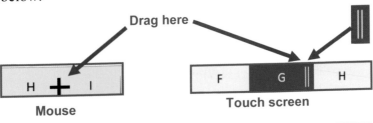

	A	B	C	D	E
	First Name	Surname	Address Line 1	Address Line 2	Address Line 3
1					
2	John	Walker	19 London Rd	Lewes	E Sussex
3	Susan	Slater	Highfield	Milfield	Stone
4	Jill	Austin	Hinckley Farm	Radbourne	Derbyshire
5	Robert	Burns	14 Belmont Rd	Murrayfield	Edinburgh
6	Sarah	Mitchell	Salmon Leap	Norham	Northumberland
7	Bob	Smith	71 Church St	Greenwich	London
8	Mike	Brunt	83 Valley Rd	Thetford	Norfolk
9	Jean	Baker	Westmead	Weaver View	Lichfield
10	Samuel	Johnson	The Cottage	Great Cubley	Ashbourne

Entering the Data

When typing the names and addresses into the cells, **don't use commas or punctuation marks** within an address field; for example, "83, Valley Rd" can cause problems.

To move down a column, press the **Enter** or **Return** key (on all versions of Excel). To move across a row to the next cell, with a mouse and keyboard, use the **Tab** key or the arrow keys. With a touch screen tap in the next cell across.

The ribbons in all the versions of Excel contain the usual text formatting tools — fonts, bold, italic, underline, alignment, text and font colours, etc., as shown below.

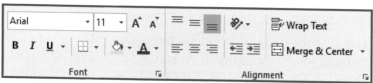

Excel 2016

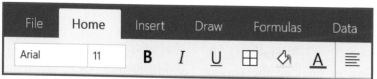

Excel Mobile

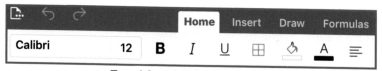

Excel for iOS (iPad and iPhone)

The Excel for Android ribbon (shown on page 50) is essentially the same as the Excel Mobile ribbon shown above. Text formatting is discussed on the next page.

Formatting the Address List

The name and address spreadsheet on page 106 was formatted as shown in part below.

	A	B	C	D
1	**First Name**	**Surname**	**Address Line 1**	**Address Line 2**
2	John	Walker	19 London Rd	Lewes
3	Susan	Slater	Highfield	Milfield
4	Jill	Austin	Hinckley Farm	Radbourne
5	Robert	Burns	14 Belmont Rd	Murrayfield
6	Sarah	Mitchell	Salmon Leap	Norham
7	Bob	Smith	71 Church St	Greenwich
8	Mike	Brunt	83 Valley Rd	Thetford
9	Jean	Baker	Westmead	Weaver View
10	Samuel	Johnson	The Cottage	Great Cubley

Selecting a Single Cell

Tap or click in the cell.

Selecting Entire Rows and Columns

Tap or click in the row or column header. Drag down or across the headers to select several rows or columns.

Selecting Groups of Cells

With a *mouse* drag the cursor across all the required cells.

Using a ***touch screen***, tap in a cell then drag the circles which appear, as shown below, to select the required group of cells.

Android   iOS (iPad and iPhone)

The icons for the formatting tools appear on the ribbons as shown on page 107. These are also discussed on page 50.

Having selected a particular group of cells, the required formatting features are applied. For example, select row **1** then select bold text and a fill colour. Then drag over cells **A2** to **B10** and select italics, bold blue text and light blue fill, for example.

Cell Borders

Various options are available for the cell borders, with different line styles and colours. Click or tap the icon shown on the right and on the ribbons on page 107.

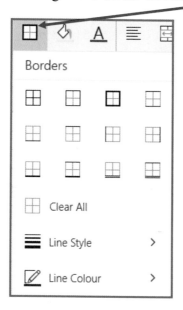

Shown above is the **Borders** menu used on Excel Mobile and Excel for Android. A similar border menu is used on the iOS (iPad and iPhone) version of Excel. A more complex menu with more options is used on Excel 2016.

Editing a Record

Using Excel for a name and address file, it's very easy to keep the records up-to-date. For example, suppose **Jill**, shown below, changed her address. Drag to select the old address as shown below.

Clear

◢	A	B	C	D	E
1	**First Name**	**Surname**	A	✂ 📋 📋 ∨ Clear Fill 🔍		
2	John	Walker	1		
3	Susan	Slater	Highfield	Milfield	Stone
4	Jill	Austin	Hinckley Farm	Radbourne	Derbyshire
5	Robert	Burns	14 Belmont Rd	Murrayfield	Edinburgh
6	Sarah	Mitchell	Salmon Leap	Norham	Northumberland
7	Bob	Smith	71 Church St	Greenwich	London
8	Mike	Brunt	83 Valley Rd	Thetford	Norfolk
9	Jean	Baker	Westmead	Weaver View	Lichfield
10	Samuel	Johnson	The Cottage	Great Cubley	Ashbourne

Then select **Clear** from the menu which pops up, as shown above, to remove the old address, as shown below.

3	Susan	Slater	Highfield	Milfield	Stone
4	Jill	Austin			
5	Robert	Burns	14 Belmont Rd	Murrayfield	Edinburgh

Then double-tap or double-click in the appropriate cell ready to start entering the new address.

3	Susan	Slater	Highfield	Milfield ·	Stone
4	Jill	Austin	Dove Cottage	Ellastone	Staffordshire
5	Robert	Burns	14 Belmont Rd	Murrayfield	Edinburgh

As discussed in Chapter 9, with **AutoSave** switched on, any changes to the file are saved automatically.

Alphabetical Sorting

To sort the records in the address file into a particular order, such as alphabetical order of **Surname**, drag over the names as described on page 108, so that they appear highlighted, as shown in yellow below. Don't include the column label or it will appear somewhere in the sorted list.

1	First Name	Surname	Address Line 1	Address Line 2	Address Line 3
2	John	Walker	19 London Rd	Lewes	E Sussex
3	Susan	Slater	Highfield	Milfield	Stone
4	Jill	Austin	Dove Cottage	Ellastone	Staffordshire
5	Robert	Burns	14 Belmont Rd	Murrayfield	Edinburgh
6	Sarah	Mitchell	Salmon Leap	Norham	Northumberland
7	Bob	Smith	71 Church St	Greenwich	London
8	Mike	Brunt	83 Valley Rd	Thetford	Norfolk
9	Jean	Baker	Westmead	Weaver View	Lichfield
10	Samuel	Johnson	The Cottage	Great Cubley	Ashbourne

Now select the **Sort Ascending** icon shown on the right and on the sections of the ribbons below.

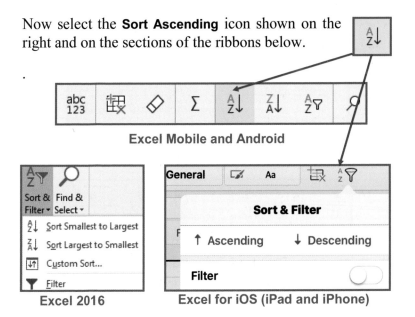

Excel Mobile and Android

Excel 2016

Excel for iOS (iPad and iPhone)

The list is displayed as shown below with all the records sorted in alphabetical order of **Surname**, shown in yellow.

◢	A	B	C	D	E
1	**First Name**	**Surname**	**Address Line 1**	**Address Line 2**	**Address Line 3**
2	*Jill*	*Austin*	*Dove Cottage*	*Ellastone*	*Staffordshire*
3	*Jean*	*Baker*	*Westmead*	*Weaver View*	*Lichfield*
4	*Mike*	*Brunt*	*83 Valley Rd*	*Thetford*	*Norfolk*
5	*Robert*	*Burns*	*14 Belmont Rd*	*Murrayfield*	*Edinburgh*
6	*Samuel*	*Johnson*	*The Cottage*	*Great Cubley*	*Ashbourne*
7	*Sarah*	*Mitchell*	*Salmon Leap*	*Norham*	*Northumberland*
8	*Susan*	*Slater*	*Highfield*	*Milfield*	*Stone*
9	*Bob*	*Smith*	*71 Church St*	*Greenwich*	*London*
10	*John*	*Walker*	*19 London Rd*	*Lewes*	*E Sussex*

Numerical Sorting

A similar method is used for numerical sorting. In the example below, the **Sort Descending** icon on the right has been used to sort students into order based on their **Average** marks in column **E**.

◢	A	B	C	D	E
1		**Maths**	**English**	**Science**	**Average**
2	John	65	86	71	74.00
3	Jill	87	92	94	91.00
4	Susan	79	63	81	74.33
5	Mike	77	59	69	68.33

Unsorted

◢	A	B	C	D	E
1		**Maths**	**English**	**Science**	**Average**
2	Jill	87	92	94	91.00
3	Susan	79	63	81	74.33
4	John	65	86	71	74.00
5	Mike	77	59	69	68.33

Sorted

Excel Filters

In a very large spreadsheet, containing many rows and columns, you may wish to temporarily remove some of the rows. The simple example below shows a to-do list for some of the steps needed to arrange a foreign holiday. For example, you might wish to display just those tasks which are still to be done. The Excel **Filter** allows you to just display certain rows while enabling you to return to the complete sheet if needed. The same methods can be used for much larger and more complex projects in a business or other organisation.

	A	B	C
1	**Task**	**Date required**	**Completed**
2	Arrange hotel	05/08/2016	Yes
3	Book flights	05/08/2016	Yes
4	Car parking	04/09/2016	No
5	Currency	07/09/2016	No
6	Print boarding passes	11/09/2016	No

Enter the tasks with suitable column headings, **Task**, etc., as shown above. The **Fill colour** icon shown on the right was used to highlight **Yes** and **No** in the **Completed** column.

Now tap or click one of the column headers, such as **Task** shown above. Next select **Sort & Filter** from the ribbon. All versions of Excel use a similar **Sort & Filter** icon as shown on the right. Finally select **Filter** or **Show Filter Buttons**. The filter buttons appear in all the column headers as shown on the next page.

Filter buttons

	A	B	C
1	**Task** ▼	**Date required** ▼	**Completed** ▼
2	Arrange hotel	05/08/2016	Yes
3	Book flights	05/08/2016	Yes
4	Car parking	04/09/2016	No
5	Currency	07/09/2016	No
6	Print boarding passes	11/09/2016	No

Tap *one* of the filter buttons **Task**, **Date required** or
Completed shown above. Tick the boxes to select the tasks
or rows to be displayed, as shown below for Excel 2016.
The mobile versions of Excel use very similar filters.

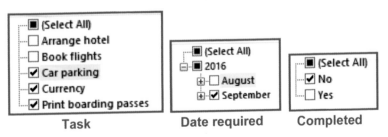

Task   Date required   Completed

In a large sheet, you might wish to use several of the filters
to select tasks or rows to be displayed

	A	B	C
1	**Task** ▼	**Date required** ▼	**Completed** ▼
4	Car parking	04/09/2016	No
5	Currency	07/09/2016	No
6	Print boarding passes	11/09/2016	No

To restore the full list, select the filter button shown
on the right and then tick **Select All** shown above.

Text Files

The *Comma Separated Variables* file (extension **.csv**) is a *text file*, which uses a *comma*, known as a *delimiter*, to separate the *fields,* i.e. pieces of data. Similar text files, (extension **.txt**), use the **Tab** key to separate the fields.

Text files, as shown below, are widely used because they are an easy way to enter and save large numbers of records. The simple structure makes text files compatible with many different types of computer system and software.

Creating a Text File

Text files can be created in a simple text editor such as **Windows Notepad**. Either the comma or the **Tab** can be used as the field separator in **Notepad**.

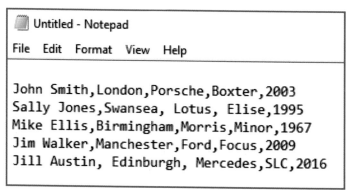

A text file created in Windows Notepad

File and **Save As** are then used to save the text file after selecting the **.txt** extension shown below.

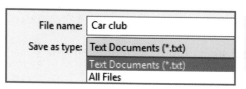

Notepad uses .txt rather than the .csv text file extension.

A word processor like Microsoft Word 2016 can also be used to create a text file. Enter the data using commas or the **Tab** key to separate the fields, then use **File** and **Save As** and select **Plain Text (*.txt)** from the drop-down menu.

You are warned that saving a Word document as a plain text file will cause pictures, formatting and objects to be lost. Apps are available for the creation of text files for iOS (iPad and iPhone) and Android tablets and smartphones.

Importing a Text File into Excel 2016

Excel 2016 can *import* text files created by other programs such as the **Notepad** file on page 115. In Excel select **File**, **Open**, **Browse**, **Text Files**, select the text file, then select **Open** and make sure the **Delimited** radio button is selected as shown below.

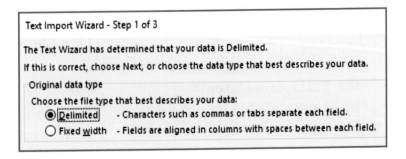

Now select **Next** and then select either **Tab** or **Comma** as shown on the next page, whichever is used as the delimiter or field separator in your text file.

Text Import Wizard - Step 2 of 3

This screen lets you set the delimiters your data contains. You can see how your text i
preview below.

Delimiters
☑ Tab
☐ Semicolon   ☐ Treat consecutive delimiters as one
☐ Comma

Text qualifier: ˙

Finally select **Next** then **General** and **Finish** to import the text file into Excel 2016, as a new worksheet shown below.

	A	B	C	D	E
1					
2	John Smith	London	Porsche	Boxter	2003
3	Sally Jones	Swansea	Lotus	Elise	1995
4	Mike Ellis	Birmingham	Morris	Minor	1967
5	Jim Walker	Manchester	Ford	Focus	2009
6	Jill Austin	Edinburgh	Mercedes	SLC	2016

A text file imported into an Excel worksheet

The new Excel worksheet can now be formatted and edited as required. Column headings could also be added.

Mobile Versions of Excel

The Excel file is then saved to **OneDrive** as discussed in Chapter 9. Then it can be viewed and edited as an Excel worksheet on any of your other computers including Android and iOS (iPad and iPhone) mobile devices.

Exporting Excel 2016 Worksheets as Text Files

An Excel worksheet can be exported as a text file for use on other computer systems and software by saving it as a text file. Select **File** and **Save as** and choose either the **.txt** or **.csv** text file extension from the drop-down menu.

Summary: Using Excel for Text

- Excel (all versions) can be used as a *database* with records such as names and addresses on separate rows. The data file can easily be edited by amending, deleting or inserting records.

- Excel has powerful formatting to make the file easy to read or to emphasise certain data.

- Records can be *sorted* into alphabetical or numerical order based on a selected column.

- Excel *filters* allow certain records or rows to be temporarily hidden from the display, e.g. to show which tasks are still to be done in a to-do list.

- The original full list of records can still be opened and displayed after using a filter.

- *Text files* are simple but very widely used files which can be produced easily on a text editor or word processor on different types of computer.

- **.csv** text files use *commas* to separate the data fields. The **Tab** key is also used as the *delimiter*. Text files may also use the **.txt** file extension.

- Text files can be *imported* into Excel 2016, saved in the **.xlsx** Excel spreadsheet file format, then viewed and edited in your mobile devices.

- Excel 2016 can *export* spreadsheets as text files using **File** and **Save As** and the **.csv** or **.txt** filename extension.

Saving Excel Files

Introduction

When you enter the data for a spreadsheet, it's stored temporarily in the *RAM* or Random Access Memory. The RAM is said to be *volatile*, which means any data is lost when the computer is switched off. With a small spreadsheet like some of the examples in this book, this might not be a problem. With a large sheet consisting of hundreds or thousands of data cells it would be a disaster, requiring many hours of work to re-enter the spreadsheet.

Therefore it's essential to *save* or copy the data to a *backing store*. Common backing storage media include the *hard disc drive* and the *SSD* (*Solid State Drive*, used especially on tablets and smartphones). Also removable storage media such as the *flash drive* (also known as the *memory stick*) and the *removable hard disc drive*.

Then the spreadsheet can be retrieved or opened in the RAM at any time in the future, when it may be edited, updated, printed or shared with other people.

Backing Up Important Spreadsheets

Spreadsheets stored on a medium such as a hard disc drive may be accidentally overwritten or deleted, or corrupted by a virus or computer malfunction. Therefore with important spreadsheets, it's been usual to make *duplicate* or *backup* copies, on a *read-only* medium such as a CD or DVD. The *OneDrive cloud storage system* discussed shortly uses professionally managed computers and acts as a backup system independent of your own computer.

Files and Folders

Files

The copy of a spreadsheet saved on a magnetic disc, etc., is known as a *file*. The file is usually given a *file name* by the user when it's saved. If not, Excel automatically gives the file a default name, such as *Book (1)*, *Book (2)*, etc. (The Excel file may comprise several sheets making up a *workbook*). Meaningful file names such as **accounts2016** obviously make it easier to find files when browsing some time later.

File Name Extensions

Files are saved with an *extension* after the file name, denoting the type of file. Standard Excel files normally use the extension **.xlsx**, as in:

address list. xlsx

Excel 2016 allows you to save files in many different *file formats*, for different purposes. These are displayed after selecting **File** and **Save As** then selecting the arrowhead shown on the right and to the left of **Save** shown below.

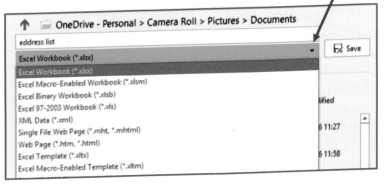

These file extensions allow the Excel spreadsheet to be exported and used in various other applications such as:

- **Web Page (*.htm, *.html)** for use on the Internet.
- **PDF (.pdf)** or *Portable Document Format*, enabling files to be opened on most computers and software.

Folders

Groups of related files are normally organized in named *folders* or storage areas. The computer folder is a virtual equivalent of the traditional wallet file or cover for loose papers. Many folders are built into operating systems such as Windows 10, Android and iOS (iPad and iPhone).

Folders can be arranged within folders, making a *hierarchy* of *folders* and *sub-folders*. For example, the Windows 10 operating system includes the cloud storage *system folder* **OneDrive**, discussed throughout this book. **OneDrive** includes, for example, the sub-folders **Camera Roll**, **Pictures** and **Documents** shown below.

OneDrive-Personal>Camera Roll>Pictures>Documents

OneDrive is also available as a free app for Android and iOS (iPad and iPhone) devices, from the Play Store and the App Store, respectively. Excel files are saved to **OneDrive** by default using **AutoSave**, discussed later in this chapter. You can also change the destination folder when saving files using **File** and **Save As**, discussed shortly.

OneDrive

OneDrive is Microsoft's *cloud storage* system where you can save your files on *Web server computers* connected to the Internet. This contrasts with *local* storage of files on the *hard disc* or *SSD (Solid State Drive)* inside your computer. The files in the clouds are then *synchronized* to any other computers on the Internet which you are signed into. So you can view and edit your Excel spreadsheets on different computers away from your home or office. These computers can include tablets and smartphones as well as laptops and desktop machines.

If you have problems with one machine the files in the clouds are still accessible from other computers. So your Excel files in the clouds, which are professionally managed, act as a secure backup system.

OneDrive is included with Windows 10 and available as a free app from the Android and iOS app stores. Users of the free OneDrive app are provided with 5GB (previously 15GB) of Web storage space. Subscribers to Microsoft Office 365 are allocated 1 Terabyte (TB) of storage, equal to 1,024GB or 1,048,576MB.

1 *TB (Terabyte)* is the storage space needed for roughly 1,000,000,000,000 letters, characters, or digits 0-9.

Other popular cloud storage systems include Google Drive, Dropbox and iCloud.

AutoSave and Save As

The various versions of Excel have an **AutoSave** option, which is usually switched on by default. This saves your files to the default folder **OneDrive** in the clouds, at regular intervals or after you make changes to the file. You can also save files to a specified folder on your computer using **File** and **Save As**. As discussed in detail Chapter 10, if you open Excel in another computer on the Internet, your **Recent** files are listed in the left-hand panel. When you select the file name, the file is opened on the computer you're currently using. It may also be available *offline*, i.e. when you're not connected to the Internet, for a limited time. However, to be certain the file can be opened offline, a copy should be manually saved on the local storage of your computer, as discussed in Chapter 10.

Saving Excel Files to OneDrive
Excel 2016

After entering the data for the sheet, select **File** and **Save As**. The **OneDrive** Internet cloud storage folder is the default destination for saving Excel files. This can be seen after selecting **File** and **Save As**, as shown on the next page, with the other available options for saving the file.

As discussed previously, saving to **OneDrive** will allow the file to be *synced* across the Internet and *downloaded* to any other computers you sign into.

Or you might choose to save your Excel 2016 files *locally on your device*, such as on the hard disc drive or SSD on your computer. These options are displayed under **This PC** shown on the next page. You can't access these local files on other computers via the clouds, i.e. **OneDrive**.

Shown below is a small spreadsheet in Excel 2016 showing athletes' times and speeds for the 100 metres sprint.

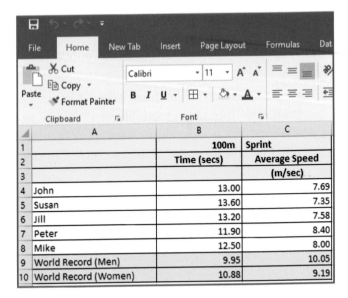

	A	B	C
1		100m	Sprint
2		Time (secs)	Average Speed
3			(m/sec)
4	John	13.00	7.69
5	Susan	13.60	7.35
6	Jill	13.20	7.58
7	Peter	11.90	8.40
8	Mike	12.50	8.00
9	World Record (Men)	9.95	10.05
10	World Record (Women)	10.88	9.19

The **Save As** screenshot shown near the top of the next page allows you to change the file name and file type.

Otherwise a default name such as **Book2** will be assigned by Excel. Then select **Save** to save the file in the standard **.xlsx** Excel spreadsheet format as shown below.

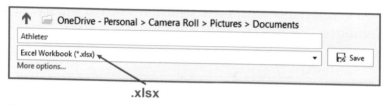

.xlsx

In this example, the file is saved to **OneDrive-Personal** in the clouds in the default **Documents** folder:

OneDrive-Personal>Camera Roll>Pictures>Documents

Closing Without Saving

If, after entering the data for the spreadsheet, you simply select **File** and **Close**, the following window appears:

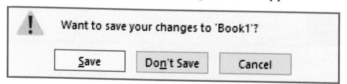

After you select **Save** and then **Save** again, the file is automatically saved to **OneDrive-Personal**, as shown above, unless you select a different location. You are also given the chance to change the file name from **Book1**.

A *local* copy of the file is also saved in the **Pictures> Documents** folder in the **OneDrive** folder on the **(C:)** drive (internal hard disc drive) in **This PC**, as shown below.

Internal hard disc drive (C:)

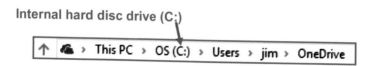

Saving in Excel for Android

In the Excel for Android version you can also use **File** and **Save As,** as discussed previously for Excel 2016, allowing you to select a destination in which to save the file such as *locally* on **This device** and give it a new name if you wish.

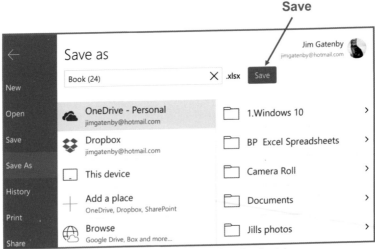

Save As on an Excel for Android

If you don't select another folder, the file will be saved to **OneDrive-Personal**, as shown above and below:

OneDrive-Personal>Camera Roll>Pictures>Documents

The **Camera Roll** folder is shown above. The **Pictures** and **Document**s and other folders can be viewed by scrolling left. When the destination folder and file name are correct select the **Save** button shown above. If you just select **Close** after entering a spreadsheet on Android, the file is automatically saved in the clouds with a default name such as **Book1**.

Saving in Excel Mobile

Select **File** and **Save** and your file is saved to **OneDrive**. Any changes are saved automatically as shown below.

A copy is also saved automatically to the local folder:

C:>Users>jim>OneDrive>Camera Roll> Pictures> Documents

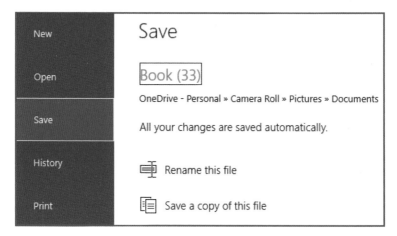

To save a copy in another location such as in a local folder, select **Save a copy of this file**. This opens the **Save As** window allowing you to change the name of the file and browse for a different destination folder.

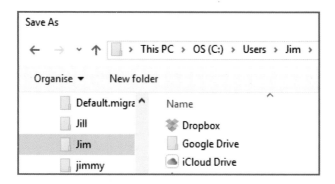

Saving in iOS (iPad and iPhone)

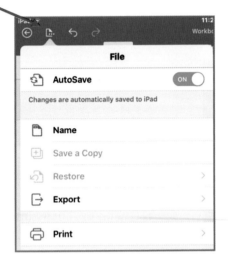

Tap the small icon shown on the left and below. The **File** menu opens as shown below.

As shown above, **AutoSave** is switched on in this example.

Tap **Name** above to open the **Save As** window shown below. Then tap **Done** and the file is saved to **OneDrive** at:

OneDrive-Personal>Camera Roll>Pictures>Documents

If you switch **AutoSave OFF**, a new **Save** option appears.

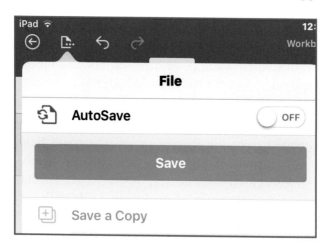

Tap this and the **Save As** window opens allowing you to enter a new name and select a new destination including **iPad**, the internal storage.

As with the other versions of Excel, when you open a file from the **OneDrive** clouds, the file is downloaded to the iPad and can be viewed and edited.

Saving Excel Files On Your Device

OneDrive enables us to access Excel and other Office files on any computer anywhere there is an Internet connection. However, you may want to access and possibly edit your **OneDrive** files where there is no Internet. For example, on a plane or after a power cut has disabled your Wi-Fi network.

As discussed earlier, files saved to **OneDrive** on the Internet are opened from the **Recent** panel in Excel. Some files may also be opened from the **Recent** panel when you have no Internet connection, if they are still in the *cache* or *temporary storage* on your device, as discussed in Chapter 10. However, to be certain of accessing a file offline, you need to actually save a copy to the local storage on your device, as discussed below.

Saving on Your Device: Excel 2016 and Mobile

Right-click or tap and hold the **OneDrive** icon on the right-hand side of the Taskbar at the bottom of the screen. You might need to click or tap the **Show hidden icons** arrowhead shown on the right.

From the menu which pops up select **Settings**, **Account** and **Choose folders**. Make sure **Sync all files and folders in my OneDrive** is ticked or tick specific folders such as **Camera Roll** and **Documents**.

Sync your OneDrive files to this PC

The files that you sync will take up space on this PC

☑ Sync all files and folders in my OneDrive

Sync these folders only

> ☑ Camera Roll (1.0 GB)

> ☑ Documents (38.1 KB)

Saving on Your Device: Android

With the spreadsheet open in Excel, select **File** and **Save as** then tap **This device** and select a folder such as **Documents** shown below.

Save

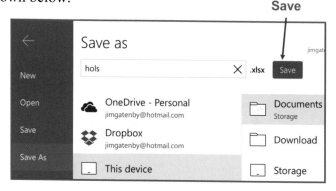

You can also give the file a new name before tapping **Save**.

Saving on Your Device: iOS (iPad and iPhone)

With the spreadsheet open in Excel, tap the icon shown on the right. If **Autosave** is **On**, tap **Name** to open the **Save As** window shown below. If **AutoSave** is **Off**, tap **Save** to open the **Save As** window. Select **iPad** shown below, enter a file name then tap **Done**. The file is saved on the internal storage of the device.

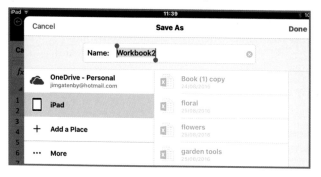

Switching AutoSave On or Off

Excel 2016

With the spreadsheet open on the screen, select **File** and **Options**, then from the **Excel Options** dialogue box, select **Save** to open the **Save workbooks** options shown below. This includes an option to set the frequency of the saving of the **AutoRecover** information, e.g. **5** minutes in the example below. To switch **AutoSav**e off, remove the tick next to **Save AutoRecover** information.

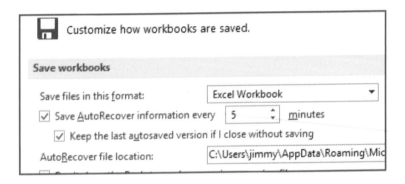

A copy is also saved automatically on the local hard disc drive storage of the Windows 10 PC. The file **Athletes**, saved in a **OneDrive** folder on the **C:** drive is shown below in the **Windows File Explorer**. In general this is:

C:users>yourname>OneDrive>CameraRoll>Pictures>Documents

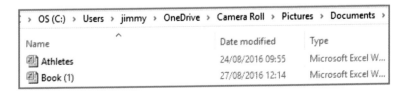

The AutoSave Location: Excel 2016

Right-click or tap and hold the **OneDrive** icon on the right-hand side of the Taskbar at the bottom of the screen. You might need to click or tap the **Show hidden icons** arrow shown on the right. Then select **Settings** and the **Auto-save** tab shown below.

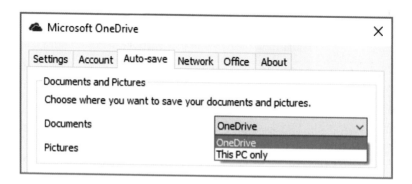

Select the **Documents** drop-down menu shown above and then select **OneDrive** to automatically save your spreadsheets in the clouds or select **This PC** only to save them on the local storage in your device.

If you select **OneDrive** above, the files are saved in the clouds in:

OneDrive>Camera Roll>Pictures>Documents

In Excel 2016 and Excel Mobile the files are also synced to your local storage and available when you're not connected to the Internet.

If you select **This PC** only, the file will only be accessible on the computer it was saved on.

AutoSave: Excel Mobile for Windows 10 Tablets

As shown below, you don't need to switch the automatic saving of files **On** in Excel mobile. To save in another location select **Save a copy of this file**.

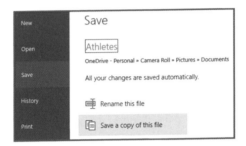

AutoSave: Excel for Android

From the **File** menu select **Save**, then drag the slider as shown below, to switch **Auto-save On** or **Off**.

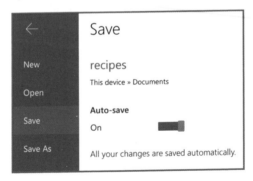

The Excel Mobile and Excel for Android **Save** menus also include an option to **Rename this file**.

AutoSave: Excel for iOS (iPad and iPhone)

Open the **File** menu and tap the **AutoSave** button shown on pages 128 and 129.

Backup Copies

As stated earlier, **OneDrive** gives a high degree of security and is itself an effective backup system. So your files will still be accessible from other computers even if your regular computer fails. Major cloud storage services like **OneDrive** have multiple server computers in different locations storing duplicate copies of your files. So the files should be protected against disasters such as fires or floods.

However, if you delete a file in **OneDrive** either deliberately or accidentally, it's deleted from the clouds and inaccessible to all of your machines. As discussed in Chapter 10, deleted files are sent to the **OneDrive Recycle Bin**. Deleted files can be *restored* from the **Recycle Bin** but only if the bin has not been *emptied* by the user or automatically after a specified time, such as up to 30 days, depending on how full it is.

So if you're working on large, important spreadsheets representing many hours of work, you may find it reassuring to make your own separate backup copies. Since **OneDrive** files can be opened and saved on many different types of computer, a variety of methods can be used to make backup copies, as listed below.

- Send copies to additional cloud storage systems, such as Dropbox, Google Drive or iCloud.

- Copy to removable media such as a read-only CD or DVD, SD card or flash drive (memory stick).

  (Some tablets and smartphones have a micro USB port allowing you to connect and save to accessories such as flash drives and SD card readers. Some tablets and phones have a built-in SD card slot.)

Summary: Saving Excel Files

- Excel spreadsheets are saved to **OneDrive** on the Internet, from where they can be retrieved for viewing and editing on any Internet computer.

- Spreadsheets are saved as *files* with a file name and usually the **.xlsx** *file name extension*.

- The files are saved in the **OneDrive** folder on the Internet by default but other destinations can be specified using **File** and **Save As**.

- The **AutoSave** option saves files at regular intervals and after changes have been made.

- A subscription to Office 365 gives additional features such as greatly increased storage on **OneDrive** on the Internet (ITB instead of 5GB).

- When you upload a file to **OneDrive** on the Internet, a copy is also saved in the *cache* or temporary internal storage on your device. The cache copy will only be available in the **Recents** panel in Excel for a limited time, such as 14 days.

- To have certain access to files *off-line*, i.e. where there is no Internet, you need to make manual copies on the internal storage of your device.

- Files permanently deleted from **OneDrive** on the Internet can no longer be accessed on any computer. For very important spreadsheets a *backup* copy on removable storage such as a CD, DVD or flash drive may be expedient.

Syncing, Managing and Sharing Files

Introduction

As stated elsewhere in this book, Excel is part of the Microsoft Office suite, which also includes Microsoft Word and the PowerPoint presentation program. Office is closely associated with the **OneDrive** cloud storage system which saves all your Excel and other files on the Internet.

This chapter covers the following topics:

- *Uploading* files to **OneDrive** from your computer.

- *Synchronising* files between different computers.

- *Managing* files in **OneDrive**, i.e. moving, copying, deleting and renaming a file.

- *Restoring* files from the **Recycle Bin**.

- *Downloading* files from **OneDrive** to local storage on your PC, tablet or smartphone, etc.

- *Sharing* Excel files with other people by copying live links to e-mails, social networks or another cloud storage system such as Dropbox .

The Overall Process

It may be helpful to reiterate here some of the main points discussed in previous chapters.

Excel files are saved to **OneDrive** by default, although you can select another folder using **Save As**, if you prefer.

When you save a file to **OneDrive**, it's *uploaded* to the metaphorical "clouds", i.e. special server computers on the Internet from where you can *download* the Excel file to any other computer you are signed into.

During the upload process, a copy of the file is saved locally on your device in a *cache*, i.e. on the hard drive, etc. This means you can access the file *offline*, i.e. where there is no Internet. However, the file only remains in the cache for a limited time and may be deleted to save space.

To be certain of offline access to a file, e.g. on a flight, you need to personally download a copy, as discussed shortly, and not rely on the temporary cached copy.

A file uploaded to the clouds is listed under **Recent** in the left-hand side of the screen, on any machine you are signed into with your Microsoft username and password.

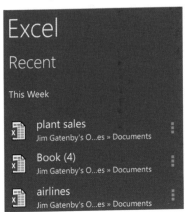

Similar Recent lists appear on Excel 2016, Excel Mobile, Excel for Android and Excel for iOS (iPad and iPhone)

If you click or tap the name of the file under **Recent**, as shown on the previous page, a copy of the file is downloaded and saved in the temporary cache on the device — laptop, desktop, tablet or smartphone.

The file can be edited on any computer you are signed into, and any changes are automatically *synced* to the clouds. You can also edit files while *offline*. Next time you go *online*, any changes made to the file while offline will be uploaded to **OneDrive**. Once a modified file is in **OneDrive**, the latest version will be *synced* to any other computers, tablets and smartphones that you are signed into.

Opening a File on More Than One Computer

If an Excel file is already open on another computer and you try to open it simultaneously on your computer, a message will be displayed, as shown below. You can still open the file but only in *read-only* mode.

Save a Copy

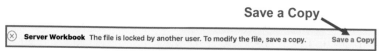

However, you can still *edit* the file if you first save a copy, as shown above, with a new name, such as **Athletes2**. Alternatively, wait for the file to be closed elsewhere.

Deleting Files

When you delete an Excel file from the clouds, it's no longer available on any machine, unless you've made a special backup copy in a separate local folder. As discussed shortly, deleting files initially moves them to the **Recycle Bin**, from where they can be recovered but only for a period of time. After this time the files are permanently deleted.

Syncing to Different Devices

The **Athletes** spreadsheet shown below was first created using Excel 2016 on a Windows PC. Then it was available almost instantly in the **Recent** panel on **OneDrive** in the clouds, on the four mobile devices shown below. As mentioned on the previous page, if you want to edit the spreadsheet while it's open on another machine, you need to select **Save a Copy** and give the file a new name.

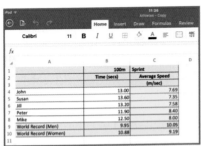

Excel for iOS (iPad)   Excel for Android (tablet)

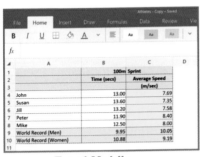

Excel Mobile
(Windows 10 tablet)

Excel for Android
(smartphone)

Despite its small size, the screen of the Android smartphone is quite legible and can be used for viewing and editing small spreadsheets.

Managing Files

As discussed on the next few pages, each of the versions of Excel have a **OneDrive** *icon* which gives direct access to your **OneDrive** folder in the clouds.

Excel 2016 and Excel Mobile

Right-click or tap and hold the **OneDrive** icon on the right-hand side of the Taskbar at the bottom of the screen. You might need to click or tap the **Show hidden icons** arrowhead shown on the right.

Navigate to the sub-folder containing your Excel files, in this case the **Documents** folder. The full *path* to the **Documents** sub-folder is shown below:

OneDrive>Camera Roll>Pictures>Documents

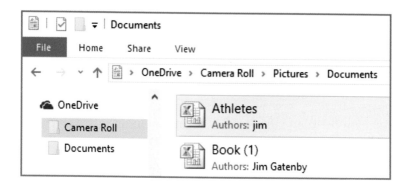

Click or tap to highlight the Excel file such as **Athletes** shown above in the **OneDrive** cloud folder.

Now right-click or tap, hold and release the file name to open the menu shown on the next page.

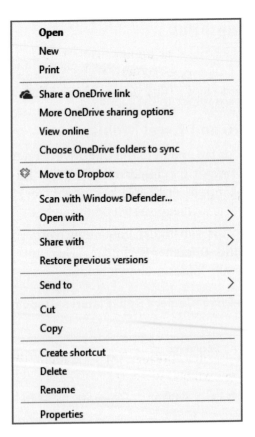

As can be seen above, the menu includes all the main options for managing files such as **Delete**, **Rename**, **Cut**, **Copy** and **Share with**. These common tasks are available on all of the versions of Excel and discussed in more detail shortly.

Deleting a file from your **OneDrive** folder in the clouds will remove it from all your computers. You might wish to make backup copies of important files on *removable storage* such as DVDs, flash drives or SD cards.

Excel for Android

OneDrive is installed as an app with an icon on the **All Apps** screen, as shown on the right. Tap the **OneDrive** icon then select **Files**, shown below, followed by **Camera Roll**, **Pictures** and **Documents**.

Files

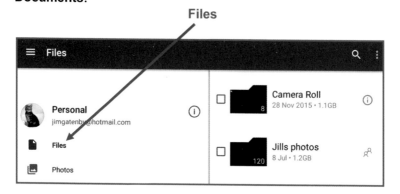

A list of Excel files appears. Tap to tick the file you wish to manage, as shown below.

Menu icons appear on the top right of the screen as shown below. These tasks are discussed in more detail shortly.

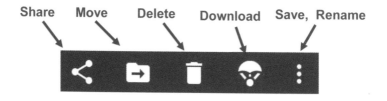

Share   Move   Delete   Download   Save, Rename

iOS (iPad and iPhone)

Tap the **OneDrive** app on the apps screen, as shown on the right. Then with **Files** selected at the bottom left of the screen, select **Camera Roll**, shown below, followed by **Pictures** and **Documents** as discussed for Android devices on the previous page.

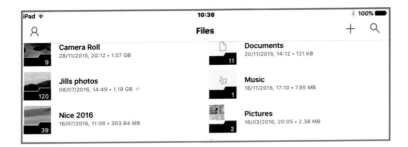

A list of files appears. Tap and hold then release to display circles for selecting with a tick the name of file you wish to manage, as shown below.

A menu bar appears along the bottom of the screen, as shown below. These options are discussed on the next few pages

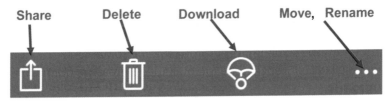

File Management Tasks in Brief

As shown on the previous pages, the same basic tasks are available on all versions of Excel. These include:

Sharing a File

Sending a link to an Excel file to other people using e-mail and social networking, with or without permission to edit.

Deleting a File

Send a copy to the **Recycle bin** from where it may be *restored* to its original folder, for a limited time, after which it is permanently removed and no longer restorable. The **Recycle bin** is discussed on the next page.

Downloading a File

Saving a copy of a file from the clouds onto the *internal storage* of your device for use offline, i.e. where there is no Internet. Not the same as the automatic *temporary storage* of files in the *cache*.

Moving a File

Transferring a file to a new folder. The original copy is removed from the original folder.

Copying a File

Placing a duplicate copy of a file in a new folder, while keeping the original copy in the original folder.

File and Save As

This allows you to save a file with a new name, while still retaining the earlier version with the original file name. The new file can be saved in the same folder or in a new folder.

Renaming a File

Changing the name of a file. The file no longer exists under the old name.

The OneDrive Recycle Bin

When you click or tap to "delete" a file, it's removed from it's folder or original location, but not permanently or irretrievably removed from the clouds. Instead it's *moved* to a special folder known as the **Recycle bin**.

Files remain in the **Recycle bin** until one of the following occurs:

- Selected files are *permanently deleted* by the user.
- The **Recycle bin** is *emptied* to save storage space.
- The file is *restored* to it's original folder.

Restoring Files

Restoring a file from the **Recycle bin** may be necessary if a file has been accidentally deleted or you've decided you need to use it again.

Permanent Deletion from the Clouds

Most files are kept in the **Recycle bin** for up to 30 days but less if the files in the bin are using a lot of your **OneDrive** allocated storage space. Once a file has been permanently deleted from the **Recycle bin**, it's no longer available at all.

Using the Recycle Bin

Windows 10 Computers

Open the Web page **onedrive.live.com**. You may need to sign in with your Microsoft e-mail address and password.

Select **Recycle bin** as shown on the next page and you are given options to **Empty recycle bin** or **Restore all items**.

If you select individual files such as **airlines.xlsx** above, the **Empty recycle bin** and **Restore all items** options shown above change to  **Delete** and **Restore** selected files.

Android Tablets and Smartphones

Tap the **OneDrive** icon shown on page 143, then tap the menu icon on the right and select **Recycle bin**. Then either tap **DELETE ALL** or select individual files and tap **Delete** or **Restore** shown below.

Android Delete   **Android Restore**

iOS (iPads and iPhones)

Open the **OneDrive** folder as discussed on page 144, then tap the human icon followed by the information icon shown on the right. Tap **View Recycle Bin** and tap and hold to select the files. Then select either **Delete** or **Restore** shown below.

iOS Delete **iOS Restore**

Sharing Excel Files
Excel 2016 and Excel Mobile (Windows 10)

Open the **OneDrive** Website at **onedrive.live.com** and select **Files** and then select with a tick the file(s) to be shared. Then select **Share**, shown below.

OneDrive Website

Then select **Get a link** or **Email** from the menu shown on the right. **Get a link** allows you to *copy* a link to your clipboard then *paste* it into an e-mail message as discussed on pages 160 and 161.

To post the link to a social network such as Facebook or

Twitter, select **More** shown above then select the icon for the social network from the list which appears. To set the permissions for the file(s) select **Anyone with this link can edit this item** as shown above and on the next page.

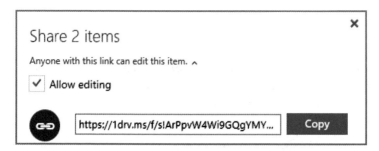

Then either tick the box to **Allow editing** or leave it blank to make the file **View only**.

If you select **Email** (page 148) a box is displayed for you to enter the e-mail addresses of recipients, add a short note and select either **Can view** or **Can edit**. Then select **Share** to post the message with the link to your file(s) in **OneDrive.**

Excel for Android and iOS (iPad and iPhone)

Select the file(s) in the **OneDrive** app as discussed on pages 143 and 144 then tap the appropriate icon as shown below.

Android
Share

iOS
Share

Available options include copying a link to e-mail and social networks with permission to view or edit the file.

Android Sharing

iOS Sharing

Summary:
Syncing, Managing and Sharing Files

- Files created or edited using any one of the versions of Excel on any type of computer can be opened on any of the other versions of Excel.

- Files created in Excel 2016 have more formatting features, etc., but the essential content of the spreadsheet can still be viewed and edited on the tablet and smartphone phone versions of Excel.

- Excel files can be edited *offline* as well as *online*. Edited files are uploaded to **OneDrive** the next time you go online and synced to any other devices.

- To edit a file which is already open on another machine, save the file with another name.

- The **OneDrive** folder and **OneDrive** Web site provide options for selecting, deleting, moving, copying, renaming, downloading and sharing files.

- The **Recycle bin** is a temporary storage area to which files are moved after a "delete" operation. Files may be *permanently deleted* from the **Recycle bin** or *restored* (within a limited time period) to their *original folder*.

- Excel files may be shared with other people by sending a live *link* to the file, via e-mail and social networking, etc. Recipients can open and *view* the file from the clouds and, depending on the *permission* you set before sending, *edit* the file.

Printing and Publishing

Introduction

Having created a spreadsheet and any associated graphs and charts, you may wish to make it available to a wider audience. For example, to distribute paper copies of a spreadsheet to colleagues for discussion in a meeting or to send out to customers an invoice printed from Excel. Or you may need to print a paper copy to file in your records in a traditional paper folder.

This chapter includes the following topics:

- Setting up a printer on desktop and laptop PCs, as well as Android and iOS (iPad and iPhone) tablets and smartphones.

- Printing spreadsheets and charts on paper.

- Printing selected cells only.

- Inserting a spreadsheet and charts as part of a document or report in a word processor.

- Positioning spreadsheets and graphs and charts within a page to suit the surrounding text.

Setting Up a Printer

If you've got a laptop or desktop PC, it's probably already set up for printing via a USB cable between the PC and the printer. It's also quite easy to connect a tablet or smartphone to a printer. The next few pages describe the setting up of printers on laptop, desktop PCs and Android and iOS tablets and smartphones.

The Inkjet Printer

These are very popular, especially with home and small business users and can be bought for under £50. Shown below is the HP Deskjet 2540 wireless printer, designed for smartphones and tablets, as well as laptop and desktop PCs.

Many printers are connected by a USB cable or wirelessly to a computer on a Wi-Fi home network. Other computers on the network can connect wirelessly to the printer.

HP Deskjet 2540 Wireless Printer
Designed for tablets and smartphones as well as laptops and desktops

As discussed shortly, most modern printers can use cloud printing services such as *Google Cloud Print*, which allows you to print across the Internet from anywhere to any printer. Also discussed is Apple's *AirPrint* wireless printing service designed for iPads and iPhones.

Microsoft Windows 10

(Applies to Excel 2016 and Excel Mobile). The same basic method is used whether the printer is connected to the computer by USB cable or wirelessly.

Right-click or tap and hold the Windows icon shown on the right, at the bottom left of the screen. Then select **Control Panel** from the pop-up menu. From the **Control Panel** select **View devices and printers** then select **Add a printer** from the top of the **Devices and Printers** window. Windows then searches for and displays any connected printers as shown below.

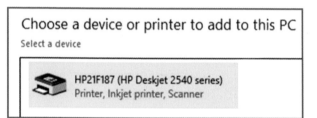

Choose a device or printer to add to this PC
Select a device

HP21F187 (HP Deskjet 2540 series)
Printer, Inkjet printer, Scanner

In the above example, the **HP Deskjet 2540** was found then selected and installed, as shown below.

You've successfully added HP21F187 (HP Deskjet 2540 series)

You are given an option to print a *test page*. Then open the **Control Panel** and select **View devices and printers** and right-click or tap and hold over the required printer in the **Devices and Printers** window. Select **Set as default printer** from the pop-up menu, to place a tick over the required default printer as shown on the right.

HP Deskjet 2540
series (Network)

Printing from Excel 2016 and Excel Mobile

Open the file in Excel then select **File** and **Print**. From the **Print** panel partly shown below, select the printer, paper size, number of copies and the paper **Orientation** such as **Portrait** or **Landscape** before selecting **Print** again to make a copy on paper.

Print Active Sheets prints the whole of the sheet you are currently working on. The **Active Sheet** appears highlighted in the tabs at the bottom left of the Excel screen, as shown on the right below.

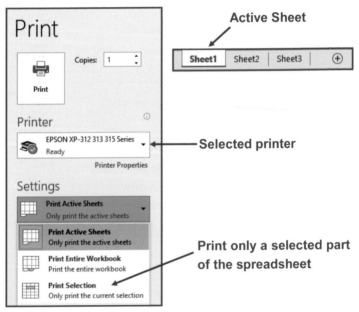

Printing Only Part of a Spreadsheet

Select the required rows, columns or cells by *dragging* as described on pages 47 and 76. Now from the **Print** panel shown above, select **Print Selection**, before selecting **Print**.

Android Devices

Google Cloud Print is a free app which allows any computer, such as an Android tablet or smartphone to print documents across the Web to any printer, anywhere.

First install the Cloud Print app on your device from the Google Play Store as shown on the right.

If you already have a *cloud ready* (Wi-Fi) printer which connects to the Web without being attached to a computer, this will be very easy to set up using the manufacturer's instructions.

A printer which is not cloud ready (i.e. not a Wi-Fi printer), is referred to as a *classic* printer. The classic printer must be connected by a cable to a laptop or desktop computer on a *Wi-Fi network with a router*. The computer must

have Google Chrome installed in order to set up the Cloud Print service as discussed below.

Open Google Chrome and make sure you are signed in with your Gmail address and password. Tap the Chrome menu button shown on the right and below and from the menu select **Settings**. Then scroll down the screen and at the bottom select **Show advanced settings**. Scroll down the next screen and under **Google Cloud Print** select **Manage** and then select the printer you wish to use.

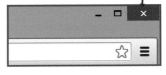

You should now see a message saying you're ready to start using the **Cloud Print** service with the current Google Account. The printer is now *registered* with **Cloud Print**.

Open the main Android **Settings** screen by swiping down from the top and tapping the **Settings** icon shown on the right and select **Printing**. You should see the **Cloud Print** service as shown below.

Tap **Cloud Print** shown above and you should see the list of printers registered with the **Cloud Print** service, as shown below. If necessary tap the green button to switch the printing service **On**.

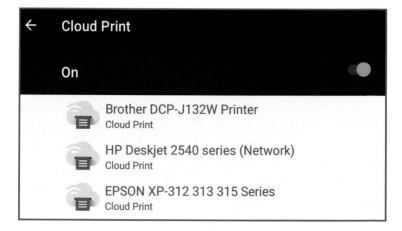

Printing from Excel for Android

With the spreadsheet open in Excel for Android, select **File** and **Print**. This opens the **Cloud Print** window on the Android tablet or smartphone, as shown below.

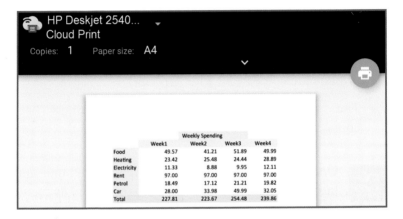

The **Cloud Print** window above includes a drop-down option to select a different cloud printer, as shown below.

You can also specify the number of copies and change the paper size, orientation (portrait or landscape) and either colour or black and white.

To print the Excel spreadsheet, tap the printer icon shown on the right and above.

Printing from iOS (iPad and iPhone)

AirPrint is a printing technology created by Apple for iPad and iPhone mobile devices. Provided you're using an up-to-date version of the iOS operating system, it requires no initial setting up. The main requirements are:

- An AirPrint-ready printer, such as the inexpensive HP Deskjet 2540 shown on page 152. (Most modern printers are compatible with AirPrint).

- The printer and your iPad or iPhone must be connected to the same wireless network.

Open the spreadsheet on your iPad or iPhone and tap the icon shown on the left, to open the **File** menu shown below.

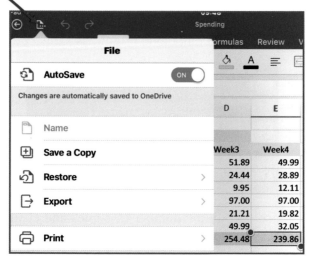

Next select **Print** shown above and then tap **AirPrint** on the small menu which appears.

This displays the **Layout Options** menu shown below, with the usual settings such as paper size, etc. There is also an option to print only the currently active worksheet, or the entire workbook, which may consist of several worksheets. The third **Print** option is to print a **Selection**, i.e. rows, columns or cells that you've selected or highlighted by dragging, as discussed on pages 47, 76 and 154.

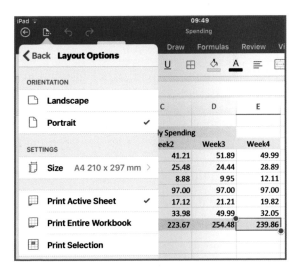

Now tap **Next** to open the **Printer Options** menu where you can, if you wish, select another of the connected printers, if available. You can also switch **Black & White** printing **On** or **Off**. Then select the number of copies and finally tap **Print**.

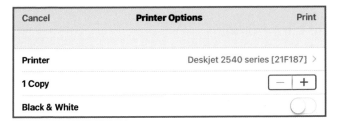

Importing a Spreadsheet into a Report

A spreadsheet and any graphs and charts can easily be inserted into a document or report in programs like MS Word. Now that versions of Excel and Word are available for tablets and smartphones, it's possible to do the work on these computers, as well as desktop PCs and laptops.

The basic method shown below is the same for all types of computer and all versions of Excel.

- Open the spreadsheet in Excel.
- Select the rows, columns, etc., to be inserted in the document, as discussed on pages 37-39 and page 76.
- Copy the selected area of the sheet as discussed below.
- Open the Word document.
- Paste the sheet onto the Word page as discussed below.
- The sheet can be moved around the page as required.

Graphs or charts can be inserted in a similar way.

Copy Command

Keyboard: **Ctrl+C** Hold down **Ctrl** key and press **C**.

Mouse: Right-click over the selected area and select **Copy**.

Touch: Tap and hold over the selected area and select **Copy**.

Paste Command

Keyboard: **Ctrl+V** Hold down **Ctrl** key and press **V**.

Mouse: Right-click over the Word page and select **Paste**.

Touch: Tap and hold over the Word page then select **Paste**.

Right-clicking a mouse produces the familiar drop-down menus with **Copy** and **Paste** options. On a touch screen, tapping, holding and releasing displays menus as shown below.

Android

iPad and iPhone

Shown below is a simple MS Word document. The table and chart were created as a spreadsheet in Excel. The spreadsheet is positioned in the document by selecting and dragging the icon shown below. The chart can be positioned by dragging, if necessary by first selecting **Format** and them **Position** in Excel 2016. Simply drag to position a chart in Excel for Android and Excel for iOS.

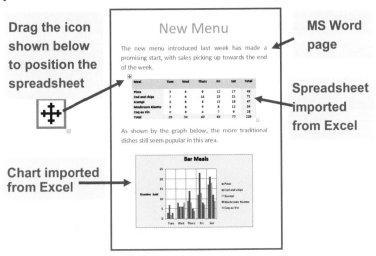

Summary: Printing and Publishing

- Inexpensive printers are available which allow you to print spreadsheets on paper for wider reading.

- Excel 2016 and Excel Mobile use MS Windows 10, which has built-in support for printing.

- Android tablets and smartphones, as well as larger computers, can use *Google Cloud Print*, to print over the Internet from any computer, anywhere.

- *AirPrint* is an Apple printing service designed to enable iOS (iPad and iPhone) devices to print over a Wi-Fi network to an *AirPrint-ready* printer.

- It's possible to print the entire spreadsheet on paper, including any graphs and charts.

- Alternatively you can print just a particular area of a spreadsheet, selected by dragging.

- A spreadsheet and any graphs and charts can be *copied* and *pasted* into a document in a word processor such as MS Word, positioned within the text then printed on paper as part of the document.

- Spreadsheets can also be pasted into the *PowerPoint* slide presentation program. PowerPoint, like Word, is now available on tablets and smartphones, as well as laptops and desktops.

- A spreadsheet can be saved as a *PDF* file and exported to most computers and software.

12

Using Excel as a Data Source

Using Excel as a Data Source

The name and address file shown on page 112 and earlier can be used to *infill* names and addresses into a *standard letter* in a word processor such as Microsoft Word 2016. It can also be used to print sticky *address labels*.

The *standard letter*, or *mail merge*, involves sending the same basic letter to many different people. Each copy of the letter is personalized, so that one letter might start "Dear Mike" while another would begin "Dear Jill", together with their corresponding addresses.

There are several stages in producing a standard letter:

- A list of names and addresses is entered into Excel and saved as a separate file in the **.xlsx** format. This file is the *data source* and can be created in any of the versions of Excel including Android and iOS.

- The basic skeleton of the letter is typed in a word processor such as Microsoft Word 2016.

- *Placeholders* or *mail merge fields* are placed on the standard letter. These are marked locations in the letter into which the name and address of each recipient will be placed on their individual copy.

- The mail merge then takes place, when the individual names and addresses are copied from the Excel file into each separate copy of the letter. Finally the individual letters are printed.

Creating the Standard Letter in Word 2016

The letter is typed in a word processor such as Word 2016, leaving space for the recipient's name and address and also a space for their name in the greeting as in **Dear *******.

With the skeleton letter open in Word, select the **Mailings** tab from the ribbon, as shown below.

Then select **Start Mail Merge** and **Step by Step Mail Merge Wizard...** from the drop-down menu which appears.

In the right-hand panel of the wizard, under **Select document type**, make sure the radio button next to **Letters** is switched on, as shown below.

Then select **Next: Starting document** at the bottom of the right-hand panel. Under **Select starting document** select **Use the current document** (since we've already prepared the standard letter and it's currently open in Word.)

Selecting the Recipients

Now select **Next: Select recipients** at the bottom of the **Mail Merge** panel under **Select starting document**.

Make sure **Use an existing list** is selected in the right-hand panel, then select **Browse....** The **Select Data Source** window opens, allowing you to search your **OneDrive** for your file, such as **address list**.

As shown in the **Select Data Source** window below, in this example, the **address list** was automatically saved in the **Documents** folder. As discussed in Chapter 9, **Documents** is a *sub-folder* within the *hierarchy* of folders in **OneDrive** as shown below.

OneDrive/Camera Roll/ Pictures/ Documents

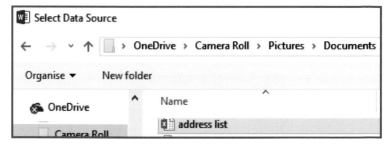

Now select the name of the required file, **address list** in this example and select the **Open** button. The **Select Table** window opens. Leave **Sheet1$** highlighted and make sure the check box against **First row of data contains column headers** is ticked.

Select **OK** in the **Select Table** window and you are presented with your list of names and addresses in the **Mail Merge Recipients** window shown in the extract below.

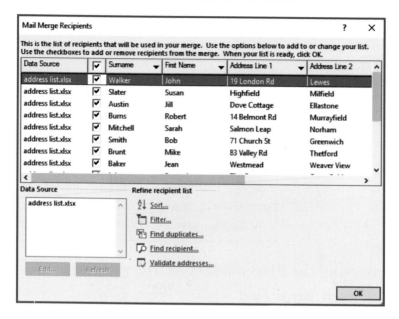

The check boxes against each name can be used to remove a recipient from the mailing list or add someone else.

Select **OK** and then select **Next: Write your letter** at the bottom right of the **Mail Merge** panel.

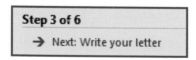

In this example we've already written the skeleton letter so we go straight on to inserting the placeholders.

From the right-hand panel select **More items...** as shown below.

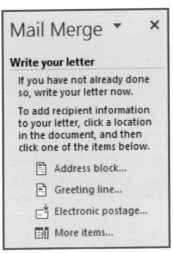

Inserting the Placeholders or Merge Fields

The **Insert Merge Field** window opens as shown below; under **Fields:** you can see that the Word mail merge facility has imported the column headings from across the top of the Excel spreadsheet, i.e. **First Name**, **Surname**, **Address Line 1**, etc.

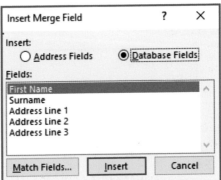

We now need to insert these placeholders or merge fields in the required positions in the skeleton letter. Place the cursor on the letter where the **First Name** is to appear and from the **Insert Merge Field** window shown on the previous page, select **First Name** and select the **Insert** button. The words **First Name** appear in the skeleton letter at the current cursor position, and are enclosed in chevrons, as shown below.

«First_Name»

Now move the cursor to the position in the letter for the next placeholder, i.e. **Surname** and select **More items...**, then select **Surname** in the **Insert Merge Field** window and finally select **Insert** to place the **Surname** merge field on the letter. Next insert the remainder of the placeholders.

Please note that each of the placeholders or merge fields within chevrons, such as **«Surname»**, can be moved, cut and pasted or deleted to give the required layout.

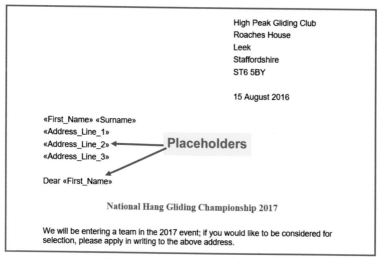

Place holders in a standard letter

Infilling the Names and Addresses

When you're happy with the placeholders, select **Next: Preview your letters** at the bottom of the right-hand panel.

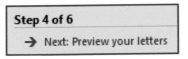

The placeholders in the standard letter are then replaced by the actual name and address of **Recipient 1** in your Excel file, **John Walker** in this example, as shown below.

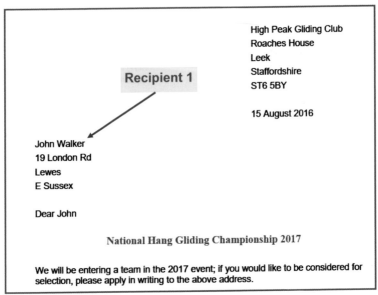

The first name and address is infilled

The **Preview your letters** panel allows you to see the letters for each recipient, by selecting the arrows shown either side of **Recipient 3** in the example below.

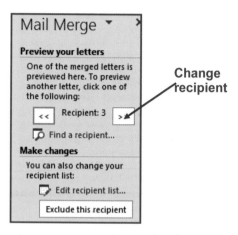

The examples below show extracts from the letters for recipients 3 and 5, with the names and addresses infilled from the Excel file shown on pages 167 and 172.

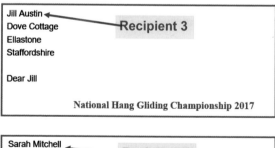

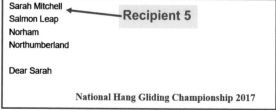

You can also **Edit recipient list...** shown below, including excluding the recipient currently displayed in the letter on the screen, as shown below and on the previous page.

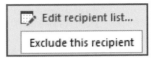

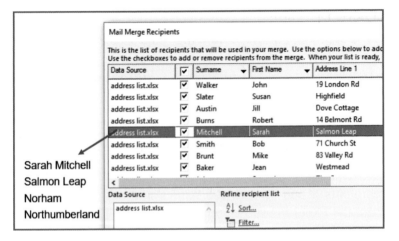

Next: Complete the merge is selected at the bottom right of the screen.

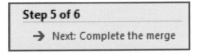

Finally select **Print...** to print all of your letters on paper, including the individual names, addresses and greetings.

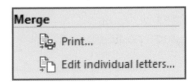

Printing Address Labels

An Excel file of names and addresses used for mailing standard letters can also be used to print address labels to stick on envelopes and parcels. These could be used for sending out newsletters, invoices or Christmas cards, for example. This can save many hours of work. The Excel file can easily be edited from time to time as some people leave or newcomers arrive.

As discussed on the following pages, the method for printing labels is similar to that just described for printing a standard letter. The main features of this method are:

- The file of names and addresses created in Excel.
- The **Mail Merge Wizard** in Word.
- Sheets of sticky labels laid out in various formats compatible with the **Mail Merge** feature in Word.

Sheets of sticky labels can be bought on A4 backing paper which can be used in a standard printer. There are various *templates* for labels, such as Avery L7163, which provides 14 labels per A4 sheet, as shown on the right. The number L7163 is entered during the Mail Merge Wizard and your names and addresses are printed to match this layout.

Avery L7163 labels

From the **Mailings** tab select **Start Mail Merge** and then **Step by Step Mail Merge Wizard...** as shown on page 165.

From the **Mail Merge** panel which appears on the right-hand side of the screen, select **Labels** also shown on page 165

Now select **Next: Starting document** at the bottom right of the screen. Then select **Change document layout**.

Choosing the Label Specification

Select **Label options...** under **Change document layout** in the **Mail Merge** panel. The **Label Options** window opens as shown below.

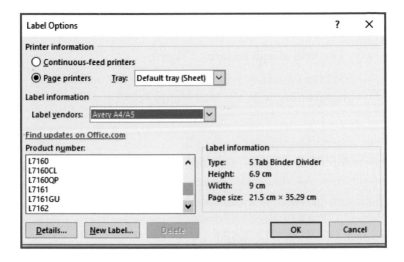

Select the manufacturer of your labels from the drop-down menu next to **Label vendors:** shown above then scroll down and select your particular labels under **Product number**.

This information appears on the packaging of the labels. Select **OK** then **Next: Select recipients** from the bottom of the right-hand panel.

Selecting the Recipients

This is the same procedure as described on pages 166 and 167 for the recipients of the standard letter.

Arranging the Layout of the Labels

Now select **Next: Arrange your labels** at the bottom right of the screen.

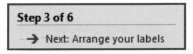

An image of an A4 sheet is displayed on the screen, as shown in the small extract below. This is ready for you to arrange the placeholders for the names and addresses.

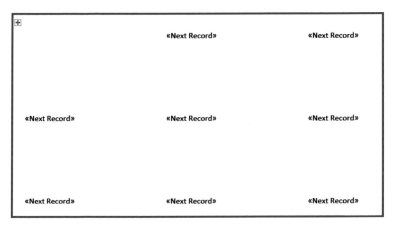

Initially you only set up the placeholders in the first label in the top left-hand corner of the page. From the **Mail Merge** panel shown on page 168 select **More items…**. The **Insert Merge Field** window opens as also shown on page 168.

Select the first field, **First Name** in this example and select **Insert** to place it on the Word page as a placeholder or merge field in the first label at the top left of the page.

Continue selecting and inserting the placeholders onto the page. Don't worry about the layout until all the placeholders for the first label are on the page. You can select the place holders and cut and paste them to move them about into your chosen layout for the labels

«First_Name»«Surname»

«Address_Line_1»

«Address_Line_2»

«Address_Line_3»

Next select **Update all labels** from the **Mail Merge** panel on the right of the screen. This will take your layout for the placeholders on the first label and apply it to every other label in the mailing. As shown in the small extract below, at this stage there are no actual names or addresses – it's just a grid of placeholders

«First_Name»«Surname»	«Next Record»«First_Name»«Surname»
«Address_Line_1»	«Address_Line_1»
«Address_Line_2»	«Address_Line_2»
«Address_Line_3»|	«Address_Line_3»
«Next Record»«First_Name»«Surname»	«Next Record»«First_Name»«Surname»
«Address_Line_1»	«Address_Line_1»
«Address_Line_2»	«Address_Line_2»
«Address_Line_3»	«Address_Line_3»

Previewing the Labels

To check that the all of the names and addresses from the Excel file are present and correct, select **Next: Preview your labels** from the bottom of the **Mail Merge** panel.

The first batch of labels is shown on the screen in the layout dictated by your chosen brand of label. In the **L1760** label format each A4 sheet has 21 labels arranged in 3 columns and 7 rows. A small sample is shown below.

JohnWalker	SusanSlater	JillAustin
19 London Rd	Highfield	Dove Cottage
Lewes	Milfield	Ellastone
E Sussex	Stone	Staffordshire
RobertBurns	SarahMitchell	BobSmith
14 Belmont Rd	Salmon Leap	71 Church St
Murrayfield	Norham	Greenwich
Edinburgh	Northumberland	London

You can scroll through all the labels by selecting the arrow buttons in the **Mail Merge** panel or make changes after selecting **Edit recipient list**....

The Mail Merge

Finally select **Next: Complete the merge** from the bottom of the **Mail Merge** panel. After completing the merge, you can select **Edit Individual Labels** if you want to make changes to personalize just some of the labels.

Printing the Labels

After previewing, merging and, if necessary, changing any individual records you are now ready to print the labels. Select **Print...** as shown at the bottom of the **Mail Merge**.

Summary: Using Excel as a Data Source

- A file created in Excel (including the mobile versions) can be used as a *data source* for infilling names and addresses into a *mail merge* feature.

- Full versions of Word such as Word 2016 have a built-in mail merge feature. This is not present in the mobile versions of Word.

- Word includes a *Step-by-Step Mail Merge Wizard* to guide you through the process.

- The titles or labels of the columns in the Excel sheet, such as **Surname**, **First Name**, etc., are used as *placeholders* in Word. These are the locations on *standard letters* or *sticky labels* in which the actual names and addresses are inserted.

- The placeholders such as **Surname**, **First Name**, etc., are arranged for the first letter or label, enclosed within chevrons. This layout is then copied to the positions of the other letters or labels.

- Sheets of labels from different manufacturers have different *Product numbers*. Microsoft Word uses this code to arrange the labels on the sheet.

- All of the letters or labels can be *previewed* with the recipients' addresses infilled, before the actual mail merge and printing takes place.

- Checkboxes allow records, i.e. names and addresses, in the original Excel file to be included or excluded from a print run of letters or labels.

Index